# The Reality of Reincarnation

When a beloved grandparent or aunt or brother dies, when we lose a parent or cherished child to death, the loss feels so sad, so final. We yearn to see them once again, to hear their voices, to feel their presence. If only we could be with them again!

Some take comfort in the belief that after we die we will be reunited with the souls of our deceased loved ones in spirit, in heaven. But what if you knew it was possible to be with them again in this lifetime without having to die first? What if I told you there is strong evidence that the souls of our loved ones who die can return from heaven to be with us again—not in a dream or vision, or through the aid of a medium or psychic, but in reality, through reincarnation as a baby born into the family?

It is possible. The true stories I share with you in this book are stunning testimony to the reality of reincarnation within the same family . . .

*Carol Bowman*

D0011581

### Also by Carol Bowman

CHILDREN'S PAST LIVES

---

# RETURN FROM HEAVEN

## BELOVED RELATIVES REINCARNATED WITHIN YOUR FAMILY

## CAROL BOWMAN

HarperTorch
*An Imprint of HarperCollinsPublishers*

HARPERTORCH
*An Imprint of* HarperCollins*Publishers*
10 East 53rd Street
New York, New York 10022-5299

First HarperTorch paperback printing: May 2003
First HarperCollins hardcover printing: April 2001

HarperCollins®, HarperTorch™, and ❦ ™ are trademarks of Harper-Collins Publishers Inc.

Printed in the United States of America

Visit HarperTorch on the World Wide Web at www.harpercollins.com

10  9  8  7  6  5  4

*Acknowledgments*

I wish to thank everyone who generously shared their stories with me and gave their permission for me to share them in this book. Without your courage and pioneering insights, I would have no stories to tell.

I also want to thank the following individuals for their help:

Pat Lawrence for taking over the task of monitoring ReincarnationForum.com, and carefully critiquing the manuscript.

Betty Ballantine for reading the manuscript and for her astute comments.

Trish MacGregor for guiding me in the writing process, keeping me on track, and for introducing me to Al.

Al Zuckerman for his perseverance and guidance.

Esther and Gregg Cohen-Eskin for doing such a fine job of being the "average reader."

Larry Ashmead for his enthusiasm, vision, and belief in this project.

Allison McCabe and Krista Stroever for their support.

And my eternal thanks to my husband and writing partner, Steve. I am indebted to him for his insight and help in shaping and organizing the ideas. I relied on his sense of composition to give this book structure and flow, and then on his superb editing skill to give it polish. I couldn't have done it without him.

# Contents

# Foreword

I will never forget the first time I held a newborn infant in my hands. I stared at his tiny hands and body in amazement. As I held him close to my heart, I was astonished at the purity and wonderment of this miracle known as birth. Nothing on earth could bring more joy. And like most people, as I stared at him, I couldn't help but contemplate his future life on this earth. Here in my arms were promise and hopes and dreams for a new generation. This was a newly formed body, but an ageless soul, and one ready to begin the dance of life, yet again.

Every soul makes its own timeless map of experiences. Lifetimes of events are imprinted into the soul memory, and all weaknesses and strengths are drawn upon for growth and understanding. Awareness forms and evolves from this knowledge, to develop our selves and incorporate them into the simple yet complex meanings of life.

Each one of us has a soul destiny, but this journey of knowledge is not traversed alone. Instead, it is shared. For we are a part of many others and we choose to come back and learn and evolve with those whom we have loved before. Though the characters, roles, and situations change, these bonds of love and familiarity are an inherent part of us. Therefore, we are our families, friends, and foes. And by sharing, learning, loving, experiencing various aspects of personalities, in multitudes of situations, we become as one in our seeking of truth and understanding.

A child is one of life's greatest teachers. Children's points of view are honest and free. Their minds have not become imprisoned and conditioned by the fears and insecurities that grip adults. A child understands simplicity and views life as a playful adventure. There is no judgment or motive behind the words of a child. They know who they are and what they want and will tell you so without your even asking.

Children are also much more in tune with their intuition. They have yet to form an awareness of a religion or belief system, therefore, they rely upon their "feelings" or "senses" to give them answers. Part of this awareness is due to the fact that they have recently arrived here from the spirit world, and their mindset is still rich with the influence of that world. Therefore utilize and nurture their light, because it is our responsibility to keep it lit. A child's mind is the seat of the soul and should be left as pure and free as possible, so they can foster a true and meaningful spiritual self. For it has been noted, one must be like a child to enter the gates of heaven.

The belief in reincarnation is found in almost every religion and civilization known to man. It was certainly part of Roman times and referred to by several ancient Greek philosophers, most notably Plato. The Egyptians' ancient religion shared a form of it as well. The belief in "coming back" and returning to this earth is just as strong today and is gaining ever more acceptance in mainstream thought. So then why is rein-carnation still a topic bathed in mystery?

In our limited, physical, three-dimensional world, there are no manmade machines that can measure the "experiences" a soul has encountered throughout time. When speaking of a soul or a consciousness or another dimension, what scientific methods can be utilized? None. As the maxim goes, it would be like trying to find a needle in a haystack.

But on another level, "consciousness" is real and tangible, as experienced through meditation, near-death, and out-of-body experiences. Consistent with these are situations where children have memories and know consistent details beyond their frame of aware-ness. Where irrational phobias and health issues were relieved by regression therapy, it also clearly demon-strates irrefutably the existence of a soul conscious-ness.

The mind is limitless. We are not our brains, our bodies, our clothes, or our homes. We are not our bank accounts, our jobs, our countries, or even our names. We are much, much more. We are spiritual beings whose true native language is love.

The time has finally come for us to open our-selves up to this new "soul awareness." That is why this book is so important, not just as an interesting story but also as a collection of lessons from which to learn and live by. When we begin to think of ourselves as eternal beings and are "conscious" of how we act out our lives on a daily basis, our lives take on a more meaningful role and we perceive the tapestry of our existence more closely. We begin to understand the meanings behind our interactions with our family, friends, and fellow workers. We start to see how our previous thoughts and actions helped to shape the life we are currently living, and we begin to live with a "mindful awareness" of every choice we make, knowing they will have repercussions far beyond tomorrow. We begin to live a life in which these very choices are not taken for granted.

This earth is the schoolroom for the soul. It is a place we come back to over and over again to further us on our road to self-awareness. We carry the hope that with all of the experiences we encounter and the variety of the scenarios we live out, we will have a greater understanding of ourselves. When we can begin to see ourselves honestly and start to assume personal responsibility, it is then and only then that we realize we are all connected as one being and behold the true meaning of God.

—James Van Praagh

## Introduction

When a beloved grandparent or aunt or brother dies, when we lose a parent or cherished child to death, the loss feels so great, so sad, so final. We yearn to see them once again, to hear their voices, to feel their presence. If only we could be with them again!

Some take comfort in the belief that after we die we will be reunited with the souls of our deceased loved ones in spirit, in heaven. But what if you knew it was possible to be with them again in this lifetime without having to die first? What if I told you there is strong evidence that the souls of our loved ones who die can return from heaven to be with us again—not in a dream or vision, or through the aid of a medium or psychic, but in reality, through reincarnation as a baby born into the family?

It is possible. The true stories I share with you in this book are stunning testimony to the reality of reincarnation within the same family: grandfathers return as their own great-grandsons, uncles return as their own nieces, mothers switch places with their daughters.

And perhaps the most amazing revelation is that children who die tragically young can return to the same mother within a few years.

All the stories in this book center around very young children, some as young as two years old, who begin talking of their past lives spontaneously, with no prompting or hypnosis. The child's family, in most cases, is a typical American family who did not believe in reincarnation before it happened to them. Yet the evidence they see coming from their own child convinces them that a deceased relative has been reborn into their family.

You will follow the process of discovery from the moment these families first suspect their child is a relative reborn. Typically, around the time the child begins to talk in full sentences, he or she will start to make shockingly accurate statements about the life of the deceased relative—facts a toddler has absolutely no way of knowing. Or the family recognizes specific behaviors in the child that mirror the relative's unique quirks and personality. In some cases they see that the child's body has birthmarks that exactly match wounds or scars the deceased relative had on his body at the time of death—marks that cannot be attributed to heredity.

I had been researching children's past lives for more than a decade when I first took notice of these special cases of *family return*. They showed me something I hadn't seen before. They demonstrate dramatically how *personal* reincarnation can be, and how emotions and relationship issues persist from one life to the next. Discovering family return deepened my understanding of reincarnation and shifted the focus of my research.

When I began investigating children's past lives in 1988, I came to it not as a researcher or even as a writer, but as a mother looking for answers for what happened with my own children. It all began one afternoon as we were sitting around the kitchen table. My daughter was triggered to remember dying long ago in a house fire, and my son gave a realistic description of dying amid the horror and chaos of a Civil War battle. I was astounded by what I heard, because at the time I had no idea children could remember their past lives. Yet what my children were saying was so realistic, so detailed, and the emotions so appropriate, I knew it was nothing they had seen on TV or overheard from adult conversation. I knew this as their mother. The clincher came a few days later when I realized that both children had been suddenly healed of chronic conditions as a result of remembering their past lives.

This was so unexpected and amazing, it opened my eyes to a whole new world of possibilities and filled me with questions. I had to know more about what had happened to my kids. And I wondered: If it could happen so naturally with them, how many other children remember their past lives too? I searched bookstores and libraries (this was in the days before the Internet) for a book that could answer my questions and tell me what to do next. In my search I discovered the work of Dr. Ian Stevenson of the University of Virginia, who has spent forty years documenting and verifying thousands of cases of children's past life memories. His incredible research confirmed that what had happened to my children was not that unusual; it is a natural phenomenon that happens to children all over the world. I was grateful to him for that. But Dr. Stevenson says nothing in his writings about practical matters—nothing about what a parent should do when a child has a past life memory. Many of my questions remained unanswered.

Since I couldn't find what I was looking for, I began doing my own research. I went to graduate school and got a degree in counseling, and I began collecting my own cases. Gradually I realized that nobody else had the material or cases I had, so I wrote a book to explain the phenomenon in plain terms and to provide useful advice for parents. I wrote the book I had been searching for since 1988 but couldn't find.

After *Children's Past Lives* was published in 1997, I began to receive hundreds of fascinating e-mails from around the world. Readers shared their own stories and thanked me for helping them understand what they were seeing in their children. They were as relieved as I had been to learn that their child's past life experiences were not uncommon and that the memories could be beneficial. As more people heard about my research from my TV and radio appearances, lectures, and Web site, the cases poured in.

I began to notice an intriguing pattern in the new cases. Many of them were about deceased relatives being reborn into the same family. I reported two cases of this type in *Children's Past Lives* and even coined the term *family return* at the time, but I thought they were the exception to the rule and didn't give them much attention. Now, from the growing number of family return cases I was seeing, I realized they deserved a closer look.

What struck me most about these family return stories was how personal and emotionally charged they are *for the parents and family*. They are not like the typical cases in my first book in which a child remembers being some unknown stranger from the remote past. The families in the new cases find themselves face-to-face with the reincarnation of a relative, a person they were close to and knew well. It is very real and immediate for them, and the emotional issues that arise have the complexity of any close relationship resumed after a long absence. For these families, reincarnation ceases to be a fuzzy metaphysical concept; instead, it comes into focus as a practical reality, something they observe and experience directly in their everyday lives.

I began to include these new cases in my lectures. Each time I did, I would hear audible gasps as people in the audience thought about their own families and suddenly realized that the child they joked about as being "just like great-grandpa" really is. Or they would be inspired simply to know that a beloved spouse, mother, child, or grandparent they missed so much could actually return to them as a new baby in the family. Some reflected on their own deaths and were comforted to know that they too might someday return to be with their loved ones again.

I discovered that these stories hold powerful lessons for *everyone,* not just parents. Some give fresh insight into metaphysical questions, such as how we choose our parents and the circumstances of our next life. Others cast a new light on the delicate issues of miscarriage and abortion. Common to all the stories is the lesson that death is *not* the end of life and that relationships continue after death by the everyday miracle of reincarnation.

Now I share these family return stories with you in hopes that they give you the same inspiration and comfort they have given others. I believe you will find, as I did, that they are rich with spiritual lessons and heartwarming surprise.

# RETURN
# FROM
# HEAVEN

# Chapter 1

## *Family Return*

Dylan was only two years old when his mother, Anne, first noticed his strange behavior. One fall evening as the light was dimming, he was in the hallway happily playing on the floor with his toys. Anne was in the kitchen making dinner when she heard him say distinctly, "I smoke too." She was surprised by this odd remark—not the usual play babble—and peeked over at Dylan, who was holding his fingers together, putting them to his lips, and withdrawing them, exactly as if he were taking a drag from a cigarette. Dylan repeated, "I smoke too." And before Anne could say anything to him, he looked over at her, patted his front pants pocket, and said, "I keep my smokes here." This puzzled her because no one in the family smoked. She couldn't think of anyone Dylan could be imitating.

Another odd thing happened shortly after that. Again it was around dinnertime when Anne was busy cooking and Dylan was playing on the floor in the hallway. He was playing with his "pogs," small cardboard disks that children like to collect. Dylan caught her attention when he blurted out, "Sevens! I'm throwing sevens!" He was on his knees, throwing the pogs like dice with a sidewise sweep of his wrist and then thrusting his little hands triumphantly into the air. He again exclaimed, "Sevens! I'm throwing sevens!"

She shook her head in puzzlement. Where did he get this? She was quite sure he had never seen anyone gamble or shoot craps in his short life. He was only two and she knew that the only TV he saw was *Sesame Street* and *Barney*. As most busy parents would, she filed this incident away in her mind, along with the one about the smokes, as a curiosity, one of the many surprises kids are prone to come up with.

But a few months later Dylan developed an extreme behavior that was not so easy to dismiss. On his third birthday someone gave him a toy gun, and from that point on he insisted on having it with him at all times. If he lost it or somebody took it away, he would throw a hysterical fit. He slept with the gun, took a bath with it, kept it in the waistband of his pants, and even tucked it into his bathing trunks at the swimming pool. It wasn't one particular toy gun he was attached to—any toy gun would do. Whenever he left the house, he had to make sure he had his gun with him. If he found he had forgotten it, he would scream until he was given another one. Once, when Dylan was taken to a funeral, he realized too late that he had forgotten it. He cried so hard it caused him to wheeze and cough. He was making such a commotion his parents had to remove him to the car. It took him a long time to settle down enough so they could drive home.

After the funeral incident, everyone in the family stashed toy guns—in their purses, in their homes, and even in the glove compartments of their vehicles—to avoid Dylan's hysterical scenes. When he turned five and was about to start school, his obsession caused real concern. The only way his mother could convince him not to take his gun with him was to tell him it was against the law to have a gun in school. Reluctantly, he obeyed.

## Pop-Pop

I first heard the story of Dylan from his aunt Jenny, Anne's sister-in-law, whom I met for the first time at a party. Jenny had just finished reading my book, *Children's Past Lives,* and was eager to talk to me about her now five-year-old nephew, who she was beginning to believe was the reincarnation of her grandfather. She explained that she had long been open to the possibility of reincarnation, but she hadn't known that it was possible for a child to be the reincarnation of a family member. Now Dylan's strange behaviors were beginning to make sense to her. She continues the story.

> Our whole family dismissed Dylan's behaviors as just amusing little things he did. We laughed about it. Nobody stopped to think there might be a cause, but by the time I finished reading your book, everything fell into place.
>
> My grandfather, who we called Pop-Pop, was a beat cop in Philadelphia during the Depression. Later he was a prison guard. He always carried a gun with him, always had a gun in his house, and always slept with a gun beside his bed. Always.
>
> During the last three years of his life, Pop-Pop was

very sick. He had been a chain-smoker all his life and was slowly dying of emphysema and heart disease. Even during his terrible illness, when he could barely breathe, he continued to smoke. In fact, the last words we heard from him as they carried him out on a stretcher were to ask for a cigarette. He died on the way to the hospital.

The strange thing is that Pop-Pop carried his cigarettes in his pants pocket just as Dylan pretended to do. Most people carry cigarettes in a breast pocket so they won't get crushed. But not Pop-Pop. And Pop-Pop loved gambling—especially dice. During the Depression he and his buddies would shoot craps behind abandoned buildings every chance they got.

After I started piecing all of this together—Dylan imitating smoking and shooting craps—I asked my mother (Pop-Pop's daughter) about Pop-Pop's last days. She told me something I hadn't heard before. One day while Pop-Pop was napping, my grandmother was cleaning the house and found Pop-Pop's gun hidden under the sofa cushion in the living room. He had moved it from its usual place on the night table. This really scared her because she was afraid that he was going to use the gun on himself to end his suffering. She called her son, who came and took the gun and threw it into the river. When Pop-Pop found out what had happened, he was furious that his gun had been taken away. I don't think he ever got over it.

When I heard my mother tell this story about the gun, my heart beat faster, I got goose bumps, and I suddenly realized, "Oh, my God—it makes so much sense! That's why Dylan has this obsession with his gun!" I am now convinced that Dylan *is* my grandfather—Dylan's great-grandfather. I believe he wants to make sure his gun remains with him at all times. He's still reacting to that incident from his former life when it was taken away from him.

As Jenny told her story, I agreed it was possible that Pop-Pop had returned as his own great-grandson. Dylan's strange behaviors, which made little sense in the context of his present family and his limited experience in this life, made perfect sense in the context of Pop-Pop's life.

In many of the cases of reincarnation I've seen, young children show behaviors and play activities that mimic their past life behaviors and habits. Dylan's obsession with guns, smoking, and craps fits the pattern. In some cases, these unusual behaviors are the parents' first clue that a child is recalling a past life. In one case, for example, a child who had been a garage mechanic in a previous life would often lie on his back under a sofa pretending to fix cars. Another little girl, believed to be the reincarnation of her grandmother, was obsessed with sewing and pretending she was a seamstress, the lifelong occupation of the deceased grandmother. These behaviors are most apparent in early childhood, up to about the age of five, when the memories of past lives are the strongest. They generally disappear between the ages of five and seven, when impressions of the past life normally begin to fade as the child becomes more absorbed in the outside world.

Getting back to the Dylan case, I asked Jenny why she thought Pop-Pop might return as the son of her sister-in-law and brother. Had they had a particularly close relationship? Was there unfinished business between them that she knew of? I explained that despite what many people think, reincarnation is not a random process. A soul may be drawn back into the same family because of strong bonds of affection, or to tend to unfinished business, among other reasons.

Jenny had been wondering about this too and she offered her conjecture:

A few years before Pop-Pop died, he and his wife moved into a duplex owned by his grandson, Dylan's father, Mike. Pop-Pop was getting old and his health was failing, so he was relieved to be able to move closer to the family. They lived there for two years. Then Mike decided he needed to sell the house to protect his investment because the neighborhood was declining. The property sold quickly, which upset Pop-Pop. His feelings were deeply hurt because he felt Mike was kicking him out of his home. Mike knew this sudden move would upset his elderly grandparents and offered to let them move in with his wife and him. But Pop-Pop would have nothing to do with it. So Mike moved his grandparents to another duplex in a nicer neighborhood.

I really don't think Pop-Pop ever got over the upsetting move.

The ironic thing is, if Pop-Pop is really back as Dylan, he's "moved in" with Mike and Anne—the very people he was mad at for turning him out. And now, as an only child, he's getting very good care! Maybe that's what they mean by karma!

## Pop-Pop's Unfinished Business

After listening to Jenny's story and the way she put together the evidence that her nephew Dylan was Pop-

Pop reborn, I was eager to talk directly to Anne and Mike, Dylan's parents. I was curious to see if they could add more details to the story and if they too believed that Pop-Pop was back. But I didn't know if they would be willing to talk to me. I have found in other cases of family return that, even though one member of the family is quite certain a relative has reincarnated among them, others in the family totally ignore the evidence that is right in front of them. They won't even discuss it, especially with someone outside the family, because the idea of reincarnation conflicts with their religious beliefs, or they believe reincarnation is superstitious nonsense. This kind of resistance is the main reason it is so hard to bring these cases to light and why, I believe, most people have never heard of family return.

Fortunately, in this case, Anne was willing to talk to me. When I called her at her home in Delaware, she was cordial, but she assured me, "There's really nothing much to talk about." She conceded, though, that she and Mike were perplexed by Dylan's odd behavior. During our long conversation she confirmed everything that Jenny had said, especially about the intensity of Dylan's obsession with toy guns. She said it sounded cute to people who heard about it, but *she* didn't think it was funny because she was the one who had to deal with his fits when he couldn't find his gun. She did admit that she was puzzled by the coincidence between Dylan's gun obsession and Pop-Pop's outrage when his gun was taken away. But, no, she didn't see how they could be connected.

When I asked her about Pop-Pop's reaction to selling the duplex, she softened and said she hoped that Pop-Pop had forgiven her and Mike about that matter, because it would break her heart to think he had died holding a grudge. Still, she didn't see a connection between her young son and Pop-Pop.

She added hesitantly: Something else was coming to mind as we talked, and she wondered if it could be related. Dylan always had a really difficult time saying good-bye to her and her husband. He would hug and kiss them over and over again and wouldn't let go, as if he were never going to see them again. Anne admitted she even hated saying this out loud because it scared her that it might be a premonition of something awful. Dylan's separation anxiety was so extreme they had taken him to a psychologist. The psychologist assured them it was nothing to worry about and Dylan would soon outgrow it. Despite the psychologist's assurances, Dylan's highly emotional good-byes still disturbed her.

Anne's remark prompted me to mention other cases of separation anxiety I have seen in the course of my work. It is quite common, I told her, in cases of both past life regression with adults and children's spontaneous memories, to find that severe separation anxiety is attributed to sudden separation or traumatic death in a previous life when there had been no time for proper good-byes.

I asked Anne where she was when Pop-Pop had died or where they said their last good-byes. She was silent for a moment, then exploded: "Oh, my God! We never went to Pop-Pop's funeral! Oh, my God! Oh, my God!"

The sudden shift in Anne's attitude was total. She continued, excited and breathless: "I never put these two things together before. We weren't with Pop-Pop when he died! The night before his funeral we went to a friend's house for dinner and Mike and our host drank some wine that had gone bad. Mike got deathly ill from it and was sick all night. I almost took him to the emergency room. Since Pop-Pop's funeral was in Philadelphia, almost two hours away, we had to call the family to tell them we couldn't make it. "Do you think that Pop-Pop was upset because we never said our good-byes?"

"Yes," I said, "it's possible."

Anne went over all of the evidence again—the toy gun, the smoking, missing the funeral—seeing them for the first time as the pieces of a puzzle that fit together to make a complete picture. It was making sense to her, not just logically, but emotionally. After she had a few minutes to process this new information, I helped her understand the full pattern by adding what I had learned from other cases of reincarnation, especially about the concept of *unfinished business.*

If we die leaving any kind of unfinished business— dying as a child in an accident or from disease, as an adult filled with anger over an unsettled dispute, as a mother leaving young children behind, or simply with concern and longing for loved ones left behind—the unfinished business travels with us when we return to Earth in another body, along with the impetus to complete or settle these issues. If we return to the same family within a relatively short period of time, we practically pick up where we left off before we died.

Families who discover they have a reincarnated relative in their midst may be able to discern what the child's unfinished business is by comparing the circumstances of the previous life—especially around the time of death—with those of the present life. They have the unique opportunity to understand some of the reasons the child came back to be with them.

In Pop-Pop's case, love and incompleteness may have drawn him back to his family. Because he felt unsettled by the move at the end of his life, and because his gun had been taken away, his soul may have been in a state of unrest. Perhaps that part of Dylan's soul needed an apology or an explanation to reach closure on that lifetime. Maybe he just needed acknowledgment to erase any doubt that he had been loved.

I described to Anne a simple technique I have used to help very young children with spontaneous memories resolve past life issues. I explained to Anne that she might be able to help Dylan with his gun obsession and separation anxiety by first acknowledging that he could be Pop-Pop reborn. She could do this by talking to Dylan as if she were talking directly to Pop-Pop and apologizing to him for the misunderstandings from the past. She could explain that they never intended to displace him by selling the house. And, she might want to address the business of the gun—how they had taken it away from him because they loved him and wanted to protect him. These words couldn't hurt Dylan in any way. If she was wrong, Dylan would simply brush them off and go on playing. If she was on target, it might actually help him.

A couple of weeks later I received a letter from Anne.

After we talked on the phone, I went downstairs to our family room to talk to Mike about our conversation. Dylan was about ten feet from us on the floor playing, appearing not to pay any attention to what I was saying. I explained everything to my husband that you and I had discussed about the gun, not saying good-bye to Pop-Pop—all of it. I also told him I was so sorry if Pop-Pop and Nanny [his wife] had been upset about our selling the duplex.

The next day, as we were leaving the house, I noticed that Dylan wasn't carrying his gun. I asked him, "Where's your gun?" because I didn't want to be halfway down the road and have to return home for it. Dylan looked at me and said, "Mommy, I don't need it anymore." And he has not carried it since. This change must have had something to do with what I told my husband the other night after I talked to you. Before that, nothing I or anyone else could say to Dylan would convince him he didn't need the gun. He *always* had to carry one—even into the swimming pool. That's how intense his obsession was! I think that by listening to our conversation, even though Dylan wasn't part of it, he just "got" it. It was instantaneous!

Now I see what was happening. I believe that Pop-Pop's soul needed to realize everything was okay. I had to acknowledge that we were going to take care of him, and I had to explain why we hadn't said goodbye to him and why the gun had been taken away. It was that simple.

I never used to think beyond this lifetime. I don't know whether it's because I was raised Catholic or what. But I really believe so much more in karma now, because I see that our actions really do affect someone else. The results of these actions can carry over into another life.

What happened with Dylan is not unique. I have documented other cases of children who found great emotional relief and even *physical* healing when a parent acknowledged their past life memories and addressed the unfinished business or other specific issues that appeared to be troubling them from the past. When there is finally closure on an issue, a burden is lifted from the child. With this resolution, the child can forget the past and become fully rooted in the present. The change can be quite sudden and noticeable, and odd behaviors and statements related to the past vanish.

Sometimes, however, it is not that simple. There may be reasons for the return of a soul that are so complex and layered they cannot be fully understood even when the past life identity is known. Simple acknowledgement might not be enough. The soul may have deeper lessons that can only be learned by traveling the full course of a lifetime and working through layers of experience. But seeing how rapidly *some* of these past life issues can be resolved suggests that a child's past life memories offer natural opportunities for healing the soul at the beginning of a life, freeing the child to develop more creatively and happily.

In several follow-up conversations with Anne, I learned that Dylan's separation anxiety did not clear up immediately, as his gun obsession had, but abated over the next year. Whether or not it was related to the life of Pop-Pop is not clear. But something else about Pop-Pop's life surfaced when Dylan was in first grade. His teacher asked each student in his class to describe his or her favorite vacation. Dylan gave a vivid and detailed description of his trip into the Grand Canyon, with its steep, winding hiking trails and red and orange rocks. He used such picturesque language in describing the natural beauty of the place that his teacher made a point of telling Anne what a wonderful job Dylan had done. Anne was totally surprised by the teacher's report because Dylan had never been to the

Grand Canyon! And since he had been to Disney World just two weeks before and had had the time of his life, it seemed even more puzzling that he didn't describe that as his favorite vacation. Anne happened to mention this curious incident to her mother-in-law, who was aware of Dylan's past life connection to her late father. She chuckled and informed Anne that Pop-Pop and his wife had once hiked into the Grand Canyon. The trip had been a high point in Pop-Pop's life and he *never* tired of talking about it.

## Dying under a Mattress

Once Dylan's family learned that children's past lives could be expressed through behaviors, his past life identity became obvious and, in the context of reincarnation, his quirky and seemingly unrelated behaviors suddenly made sense. By opening themselves to the idea of family return, they were able to reap two priceless benefits: they got to the root of Dylan's annoying behavior, and they were able to make up with Pop-Pop even though he had died years before.

Behaviors were the primary clues in Dylan's story. Statements are another way a child reveals a past life identity. When a child speaks with uncanny accuracy about the details and events of a deceased family member's life—things the toddler could not possibly have learned—it can be a sign of reincarnation.

The next story is an example of this. A little boy shocked his mother, Tracy, when he described the details of a family tragedy that no one in the family dared talk about. Tracy described what happened to me during a phone interview.

Because I was only two years old in 1970 when my family's house burned to the ground, I have no memory of it. All I knew until recently was that it happened on a very cold night—we live in upstate Michigan, where it gets very cold—and that my parents, five of my six brothers, and I managed to get out of the house in time. My father ran back into the burning house to rescue my three-year-old brother, Gary, but he got trapped in the house and both he and Gary died in the fire. No one in the family ever talked about it because my mother was so devastated from losing my father and youngest brother. Everyone in the family knew it was taboo even to mention it.

I have no memory of that horrible night, but my son, Peter, who was born in 1990, knew all about it. It started when he was three and the night terrors began. Peter would wake up in the middle of the night screaming, "Mommy, Mommy, Mommy!" Each time when I ran into his room, I was shocked by his bizarre behavior. He seemed to be awake, because he was sitting up and staring straight ahead with his eyes wide open. But when I asked him what was wrong, he pushed me away and yelled, "Go away! I want my mommy, I want my mommy!" Nothing I did could calm him down. He would just scream louder and push me away as if he didn't know who I was. These episodes went on for several long months, exhausting me emotionally and physically.

Around the same time that the night terrors began, during the day when Peter was awake, he began telling me stories about his "friend" Gary and how he died. He talked about Gary all the time and especially about the night Gary's family was awakened by the barking of their dog to find the house on fire. He described the house, always calling it the "yellow house." He said it had a big pine tree next to it that burned too, and a driveway that made a circle in front of the house, not like our driveway. He added that Gary's grandparents, who lived across the road, ran over and stood outside in the cold with the family watching helplessly as the house burned. He described the three fire trucks that came with their lights flashing and one big fireman with a brown beard. He talked about the fire often, adding a little more detail each time. He seemed to be able to see the whole scene in his memory, and knew exactly what was going on both inside and outside the house at the same time.

Peter was describing details that I had never heard before. Every time he told more of the story, I called my mother, Edith, to see if he was right and not just making it up. Each time, Edith confirmed that every detail Peter gave was correct. The circular driveway, the burning pine tree, grandparents, barking dog, and fireman with the beard—all were accurate.

If that wasn't weird enough, what really chilled me was that little Peter described how Gary and his father died. He said that when his father ran back into the house to save Gary, they were blocked by the flames and couldn't get out, so they hid under a mattress to get away from the smoke. I didn't want to ask my mother about this awful detail, so I asked my oldest brother. He said it was true. The firemen had found both bodies under a mattress.

I started to suspect that Peter might be the reincarnation of Gary. But I tried to find another explanation because nobody I know believes in reincarnation. I thought it was *possible* that Peter could have been really lucky and imagined all the correct details. But I didn't see any way a three-year-old could imagine hiding and dying under a mattress. That's when I started thinking seriously that Peter was the reincarnation of Gary.

Peter repeated the story of the fire, always with the same details, for about a year until he was four. The memories always came up spontaneously and randomly, with nothing I could see to trigger them. For example, he would be playing on the floor with his toys and suddenly stop playing, stare at me, and with a very serious expression tell me again about the dog barking and the brown-bearded fireman and the smoke and hiding under the mattress. When he talked about the fire, his demeanor changed completely. Usually he was a carefree child, so happy and bubbly everyone called him "Silly." But when he spoke of the fire, he became serious and focused hard on the images in his mind. If I got up to move or do something else while he was talking about it, he would follow me around to make sure I was listening. Clearly, he had something important to tell me and he wanted my attention.

Peter's accurate descriptions, his changed demeanor, and the fact that his memories dwelled on his traumatic death are consistent with patterns I've found in children's past life memories in general. When young children speak of a past life, their tone becomes serious, matter-of-fact, and does not resemble the sing-songy, lilting style of fantasy babble. Their countenance becomes calm, almost adultlike. Unlike the stories of a child who is fantasizing, these past life stories remain consistent in detail over time—sometimes for weeks, months, even a couple of years. As a child's vocabulary increases and he is better able to express himself, the story may be filled in with more refined details, but the gist of it remains the same.

When children recall their past lives, they often describe events surrounding their most recent deaths, especially if the deaths were traumatic, as in Peter's case. To the parents' amazement, a child will matter-of-factly tell them she remembers being shot, or dying in a car accident or in a war, and sometimes will add explicit and clinically graphic detail. In this case, Peter knew that Gary and his father had huddled under a mattress to protect themselves from the fire—something a three-year-old could never imagine. This kind of accurate detail is often what first alerts adults to a past life memory in a child.

Peter's mother, Tracy, found an opportunity to test her son's memory. Edith had a photograph of the whole family taken shortly before Gary's death. It was one of the few belongings that survived the fire and, curiously, it survived a second house fire some years later as well. Tracy showed the photograph to Peter and he immediately pointed to Gary and said, "That's my friend Gary." He couldn't identify any of the other five brothers, only Gary. Tracy could see from the photo that Peter and Gary looked alike, almost like identical twins. None of the other boys resembled Peter nearly as much.

Another behavior that Tracy believes stems from the tragedy is Peter's hysterical fear of fire. If a cigarette is lit in front of him, he panics and runs away. If he sees a lighter, he'll "just flip out." He doesn't like woodstoves, either, and the sight of Edith's kerosene heater makes him go berserk.

No one knows how the fire that killed Gary started. But from what we know of the workings of past life memories in general, his phobia of anything that could start a fire is understandable. There are hundreds of documented cases of young children with phobias that stemmed from the way they died in a past life, especially if the death was sudden or traumatic. For example, I have in my files several cases of babies who cried hysterically whenever an airplane flew overhead. When they were old enough to talk, and saw an airplane, they warned their parents to hide because they remembered *when they were big before* and the bombs from the airplanes killed them. Phobias can be very specific and seemingly strange and bewildering to the parents, who see no connection to anything that happened to the child in this life. But if the child remembers how he died in a past life, the correspondence between the mode of death and the phobia suddenly becomes quite clear. In cases of same-family reincarnation where the facts of the previous incarnation are known, parents can easily trace the origin of the phobia.

Besides the many accurate statements Peter made about the fire, his grandmother, Edith, observed that some aspects of his personality were identical to Gary's. Gary had been extremely shy and clingy around strangers, not outgoing at all. So was Peter. Although shy, Gary was protective of his mother: No one could say a bad word around Edith without Gary jumping in to defend her. Peter was the same with Tracy. Both Gary and Peter had speech problems and were difficult to understand. Peter, who is now ten, is just finishing speech therapy.

These similarities in personality and Peter's uncanny knowledge of the fire scared his grandmother. Not only did Peter seem to know everything about that night, he always described it from Gary's unique perspective. It was just too eerie! Edith tried to find a logical explanation for what was happening with her grandson, and the only one she could come up with was reincarnation—something she had never believed in before.

Shortly after Peter began speaking about the fire, Tracy encouraged Edith to question him directly. Edith asked questions and Peter gave correct answers. From the time they began having these chats, Peter no longer mentioned the fire to Tracy, but would only talk about it in private with his grandmother. These conversations convinced Edith, to her great relief, that Peter was Gary reborn. For the first time in more than twenty years, she was able to talk about the fire with her family, and for the first time in twenty years, she was able to mention her dead son by name.

Once Edith started to open up and talk about the tragedy, she revealed a painful secret to Tracy, a secret she had swallowed and kept inside her all these years since Gary's death. As Tracy told me:

> My mother never spanked us—ever—no matter what we did. I found out only recently that the reason she never spanked us is because the night Gary died, right before he went to bed, she had spanked him for something he had done. Then he died. Not only did she not have a chance to say good-bye to him before he died, but her last act was a punishment. If only she had sent him off to bed with a kiss and an "I love you!" She felt so guilty about this, that's why she couldn't bear to talk about the fire with anyone for all of these years— until Peter brought it up. (He never said anything about the spanking incident, though.) But now that my

mom has finally revealed this to me, she goes on and on about it. It must have increased the torment of Gary's death, and she kept it all bottled up inside. It makes me feel good to know she got a second chance and doesn't have to carry that guilt around anymore. Now that Gary is back, she can let go of it. She's free.

I believe that's why Gary came back. He came back to be with my mother again and to help her heal from that terrible tragedy long ago. I can see that the two of them have a natural closeness and easiness with each other that must come from their having been mother and son before. Their bond is so strong that sometimes she slips up and calls him "son," and in return he calls her "mom." Whenever Peter is really troubled about something now, he won't talk to me about it. He'll go to my mother first. I would feel very left out as his mother if I didn't understand that he is Gary reborn and that he needs to have this special relationship with her.

Tracy understood why Gary came back to be with Edith, but why, she wondered, did he come back as *her* child? After all, Edith had five other children. She guesses he chose to be her child for both emotional and geographic reasons. Being the only daughter, Tracy was the closest to her mother emotionally; and since they lived nearby, Peter would have the opportunity to regularly spend time with Edith. In retrospect, Tracy finds it interesting, too, that Edith insisted on being present at Peter's birth—the only birth she ever wanted to attend of all her many grandchildren. Perhaps, on some level, Edith sensed that this was going to be a special grandchild. Of all of the grandchildren, Peter is her favorite.

Peter's past life memories changed Tracy deeply. Coming to terms with the fact that her dead brother and her son are somehow the same has expanded her inner life, giving her comfort, hope, and a yearning to learn more about the world of spirit. But it hasn't made her outer life easier. She's surprised at the resistance and hostility she encounters from others.

I believe that Peter is the reincarnation of Gary. But I wanted help understanding what that means. I went to priests and ministers for advice, to ask them what was happening with my son. But they all turned me away. They thought that I was nuts and had a problem. My mom believes what I believe, that Gary is reborn. But my husband doesn't. The rest of the family tells me to "get off it." They refuse to believe what's right in front of them.

# Chapter 2

## A Child Reborn

*How do you accept that your own child who died is back in a new body? Sometimes I get a very high feeling—I feel like I'm walking on air. Other times it's hard to believe, and I probably wouldn't be human if I didn't have some doubt in my mind somewhere. It's so overwhelming because it's forcing me to look at life and death differently. Nothing less.*

Kathy was sixteen years old when her son James was born in March of 1978. She wasn't married and had distanced herself from James's father, who was an ill-tempered young man. Kathy never saw him after they split up, and he never saw his own son. Alienated from her own parents, Kathy moved into her own apartment and completely devoted herself to caring for James. He was a delightfully good-natured child with beautiful, curly blond hair like his father's. Kathy put her plans to finish high school on hold.

Shortly after James started to walk, around sixteen

months, Kathy noticed he was limping. One day he fell down on the living-room floor and couldn't get up. When he tried to put weight on his left leg, he cried out in pain. Kathy immediately took him to the doctor and an X ray showed James had a fracture of his left leg. The doctor also noticed a lump, a nodule, above his right ear. Further tests were ordered. Kathy was stunned when the test results came back. The radiological examination and biopsies of the nodule above his right ear and the bone-marrow test revealed that James had a neuroblastoma with metastases—a form of tumorous cancer that is often fatal for young children.

Kathy was devastated. A long series of radiation and chemotherapy treatments was begun in an attempt to shrink the tumors that were spreading all over James's body. As a side effect of the treatments, all of his beautiful curls fell out. Kathy devotedly cared for her little son while clinging to hope of a cure. She simply refused to believe that he could die.

But James's fragile two-year-old body, assaulted by disease and chemotherapy treatments, weakened further because he couldn't keep food down. In an attempt to sustain him, the doctors placed an IV in his right jugular vein. The incision left a linear scar on James's neck. After this round of treatments, Kathy took him home. Her life now centered around James's disease and his care—far from the usual concerns of most eighteen-year-old girls.

A few months later James was readmitted to the hospital because of excessive bleeding from tumors in his mouth. He also had a large tumor behind his left eye that made him blind in that eye and visibly distorted the left side of his face. Sadly, this time the doctors concluded they could do nothing more for him.

Kathy took him home again, knowing that he was dying. Her mother and family, for the first time in years, came to Kathy's aid and rallied to help her care for James.

Kathy explained to me the utter helplessness she felt at the time: "Usually when a child is sick, you give them medicine for fever or for an earache, and you can help control the illness until they get better. For seven months I denied the possibility that James could die. I had always felt that through the Lord and me we could stop the illness. But when the doctors told me there was nothing more they could do, my hands were tied. All I could do was sit there and watch him die. It was devastating to find out he had a fatal disease, but it was even worse to sit and watch him die, knowing there was nothing I could do. Not a thing."

Sometimes, when Kathy saw James cry, she would go off by herself to another room in the apartment and weep. When James saw this, he would get upset with her and say, "Mommy, don't cry anymore." On the morning of April 10, 1980, two-year-old James told his mother one last time, "Don't cry for me." Then he died.

Honoring her dying son's last wish, Kathy held back her grief. The reactions of her family made her stifle her feelings even more. "I saw that everyone around me was falling apart emotionally. Someone had to be the strong one, so I could never let myself go. I had to be the backbone of the family and I felt cheated of my emotions. I needed someone to take care of me, but everyone else was so wrapped up in how they were feeling there was no one there for me. It got to the point where I didn't want to listen to how they felt; I just couldn't bear to hear it. So I disconnected from myself and everyone else. I should have been angry, I should have been sad. But I bottled up all of my feelings and just kept walking."

To add to her misery, Kathy's own mother accused her of not loving James because she didn't show her grief. Although Kathy understood that her mother's anger was misplaced and that she was terribly upset at the loss of her grandson, the accusation made the rift between them wider than it ever had been in the past.

## Something Big and Powerful

Kathy had no choice but to pull herself together and get on with her life. Eventually, she married Don, a friend she had known when James was alive, and they soon had a daughter, Katie. But the marriage lasted only four years and ended in divorce. Kathy again found herself alone raising a young child. Still a young woman in her early twenties, she had responsibilities and experiences that belied her years. As she put it, "I grew up fast."

A few years later she met and married Billy, a former rodeo champ and ex–navy man. With Katie, they moved out of Chicago to a town in northern Illinois, and in 1987 they had their first child together, a son they named Josh. Finally in a good relationship and blessed with an adorable daughter and a wonderful new baby, Kathy's world was looking brighter. Billy knew about James and Kathy's painful past, and he honored Kathy's wish never to mention him or his death to their new family. Kathy never wanted to look back.

Although her experience with James had left a deep wound in her heart, it also taught her to cherish each day of her life and every moment with her family. "I learned a lesson from James that was a turning point for me: not to take a child's life for granted (as so many people do) because he or she may be here only for a short time. We never know. Because today could be the last day I see one of my kids, there are always lots of hugs, kisses, and *I love you*s in our house."

In 1992 Kathy was delighted to learn she was pregnant again. In late December the baby was delivered by cesarean section. While she was still groggy from the anesthetic, a group of white-coated specialists filed into her room. One of the doctors solemnly addressed her: "Has your husband told you yet?" Kathy's heart sank down to her toes. In that instant she was sure her baby had died.

The doctor continued, "You have a new son. But we need to warn you before we bring the baby in that he has no color in his left eye. His right eye is normal, but we think he is totally blind in the left eye."

Although most mothers would have been terribly distressed by this news, Kathy was relieved and happy just to know that her baby was alive. She thought immediately about the name she had picked out. She would name him Chad.

But the news about the eye was just a prelude. Nothing could have prepared Kathy for what followed when the nurses brought the baby in. The moment she laid eyes on Chad, she noticed a dark, slanting birthmark on the right side of his neck exactly where the IV incision had been on James! She asked one of the doctors, the pediatrician, about the scarlike mark on the baby's neck. She wanted to know how such a thing could possibly have happened. He dismissed it by saying, "It's just a birthmark." But Kathy wasn't convinced. It didn't look like a birthmark to her; it looked like a scar. It was too deep to be a nail scratch and it wasn't an open wound. It was a straight line, like a surgical scar. The incision on James had also been a straight line that hadn't required stitches. Now here was the same mark on Chad. She quickly checked him from head to toe and saw that he also had a cyst on the right side of his head one inch behind his ear—the very place where doctors had removed tissue for a biopsy of James's tumor. She asked another doctor in the group crowded in her room about the cyst. Was it a tumor? She had to know! He said it was a benign cyst that would go away in a few weeks.

Kathy was spooked by these "coincidental" marks on Chad's body. She thought back to how James looked before he died, how anybody could tell he was sick from those three things: the opaque eye from his blindness, the scar on his neck, and the tumor above his right ear. Here were the very same marks on Chad. Then the realization hit. As she held him for the first time, an ocean of relief washed over her. Instantly she knew that something big and powerful was happening to her.

"It was as if a great weight lifted from my soul," she told me later. "I suddenly felt at ease, finally at peace. Before that moment there was always something missing in my life. But in that moment the hole was filled: I felt that James was back. All of this was happening to me as the doctors were rambling on and on about Chad being blind in one eye. I didn't care. I was completely taken over by this powerful feeling and the bond I felt with Chad. It was as if we had been connected before and I could sense it and feel it. I felt totally blessed."

Kathy knew she couldn't tell anyone what she was

feeling. The doctors would *never* understand. Her family would be skeptical. But she was certain that what she was experiencing was not wishful thinking or a fantasy that grew from longing for her dead son. It went beyond that—beyond anything she had known. "When my other children were born, I still longed for James. When Josh was born, since he was a boy, I looked for any resemblance to James. There was none at all. And when Katie was born, there was no resemblance to James. I love them just as much for who they are. But as soon as I saw Chad, it was different. I could see it and I could *feel* it the first time I held him. I had this feeling that went straight into my heart. I knew he was James. It gave me so much comfort to know he had come back to me."

It took Kathy six months to muster the courage to admit to her husband, who had never known James, what she suspected about James and Chad. Billy agreed there was something different about Chad, and he saw Kathy's special bond with him, but beyond that, he didn't know what to think. Kathy's mother, grandmother, and an aunt who had known James were amazed by the similarities between the two babies, but they never spoke their thoughts aloud. One aunt later admitted that she could *feel* James in Chad, but was initially afraid to discuss it with Kathy for fear of opening old wounds.

But not everyone in the family was as open to the possibility that James was back. When Kathy mentioned the physical similarities between baby Chad and James to her ex-husband, Don, who had also known James, he told her she had lost her mind. Kathy learned to keep her thoughts and feelings to herself.

As Chad grew and his personality developed,

Kathy's side of the family noticed more similarities between the two children. Chad is quiet, soft-spoken, and nervous, just as James had been. Chad "throws" his left leg when he walks, favoring his right one; James had had significant tumors in his fractured left leg, so he limped. Kathy compared pictures of the two boys at the same age and noticed that James's tumor had made the left side of his face shorter than the right. The left side of Chad's face is also slightly shorter than the right. It is as if that side of his face is frozen in time. Chad's coloring is also very light, like James's, and he stands out in the family because all of Kathy's other children are dark. James's father was fair, with blond hair and blue eyes, while Chad's father has black hair and dark brown eyes. Kathy too is dark, with dark brown hair and green eyes. So Chad resembles James in coloring, but does not resemble the rest of his family.

Kathy's sister observed another striking similarity. By the time Chad was four, his baby teeth had deteriorated. The pediatrician blamed it on bottle-feeding, but Kathy pointed out that her other three children hadn't had this problem and they too were bottle-fed. She wondered if the deterioration of Chad's teeth could be another physical carryover from James, who had more than a dozen tumors in his mouth when he died.

To add to the mystery, Kathy took Chad to specialists all over Chicago to find a cause and cure for his blindness. But the doctors couldn't determine why he was blind in the first place—they couldn't find any medical reason for it at all. When they examined him they found that his left eye was completely unresponsive and had no tearing reflex when they shined a light on it. The only diagnosis they could give was corneal leukoma or "separation of the retina." Kathy was certain that this condition had something to do with James because the tumor had caused his eye to protrude and disconnect from the retina. But she knew she couldn't share this with these medical experts—they would think she was daft.

## "Because I Left You There"

The fullness and quick pace of Kathy's life left little time for her to ponder the mystery she lived with daily. She gave birth to another daughter two years after Chad was born, and along with raising four kids she worked full-time as the nightshift manager at a Dunkin' Donuts. Billy worked at the local Motorola plant and moonlighted at a gas station.

In early 1997, when Chad was four, the mystery again moved to the forefront of Kathy's life. Chad started remembering things. One day, quite out of the blue, he asked his mother if she remembered their "other" house. Taken aback, Kathy asked him, "What *other* house?" He described the house as being orange and brown outside with "chocolate" furniture. He then asked for his toys, including a red "weeble-wobble" toy that jingled when it rolled. Kathy didn't respond directly to his question but turned it around, hoping to get more information from him. She asked, "Why do you want to go back to this other house? For the toys?" He looked her straight in the eye and said, *"Because I left you there."*

These words made the hair on the back of her neck stand up. The house Chad described was the apartment where she and James had lived when he was a baby. It was orange-and-brown stucco brick on the outside, and they did have brown, "chocolate-colored" furniture. The weeble-wobble toy had indeed belonged to James; neither Chad nor his older brother had ever owned one. Kathy knew she hadn't mentioned these details to Chad and neither had her husband Billy, who had not known James and had never seen the apartment building. She didn't have any photos of her apartment or its interior. Chad's last remark, *"because I left you there,"* was the first indication that he identified with James. Although Kathy had sensed the connection from birth, until that moment she had never dreamed that Chad himself knew.

And he didn't say it just once. Over the next few months Chad repeatedly implored her to take him to the other house. Whenever he talked about it, Kathy got goose bumps all over. She also noticed that when Chad spoke of James's life, his tone and his countenance were markedly different than usual. "When Chad tells a tall tale, he looks away and has a mousy voice. But when he slips into these conversations about the other house, he has a totally different expression. He looks me straight in the eye and uses a strong, no-nonsense voice. I can feel his sincerity."

Kathy didn't know what to do. She deflected Chad's questions and requests to go to the other house because she was afraid to find out the truth. She explains her state: "I should probably see if the place is even still there and take him there. It's really not that far in miles, but in butterflies and nerves, it's far! What if it *isn't* the place he's talking about? Or what if it *is*?"

Once, when Kathy evaded Chad's request, he became so frustrated with her that he clenched his hand into a fist and exploded, "Mom, this is not in my mind, it's true! Why don't you call your dad and ask him where I lived. Because *he* knows." Kathy adds, "The weird thing is that Chad doesn't know my dad at all, but Dad lives near that apartment and near where James is buried."

Now that Chad was remembering his former life, the strong emotions Kathy had pushed deep down inside her for seventeen years were welling up again. These sudden intrusions of feeling surprised her and, at times, were overwhelming. "Doctors try to prepare you to give birth to a child, but mentally they can't. You can take all of the childbirth classes you want, but you're still not prepared for it. And you're definitely not prepared to hear that your child is going to die. Even if you hear it on a daily basis, you can't accept it. And then how do you accept hearing that this child is back? Sometimes it's a very high feeling—I feel like I'm walking on air. Other times it's hard to believe, and I probably wouldn't be human if I didn't have some doubt in my mind somewhere. If Chad talked about being a person in a past life in some distant time, or someone who had been a stranger to me, it wouldn't be as emotional. But these two children, James and Chad, both belong to me. This is so overwhelming because it's forcing me to look at life and death differently. Nothing less."

Kathy wrestled with her own feelings and her reluctance to face Chad's memory head-on, but she also knew she wasn't the only one struggling with this. Chad was too. From what he was saying and the way he was saying it, she could sense he needed to settle something in his mind, in his *soul*, from his former life. "I think right now Chad is looking for help and I don't know how to help him. When he's talking about this, he'll look at me like he's confused. I know he wants to go back—but does he just want to see the house again, or is it more? At times it gives me a sick and uneasy feeling because I don't know what to do." Kathy prayed to find someone to help her understand what was happening with Chad.

## Same Soul, New Body

A few months later Kathy was in a bookstore and my book, *Children's Past Lives,* seemed to fly off the shelf at her. She was excited to find the help she was looking for. Before she even got past the first chapter, she copied down my e-mail address from the back of the book and gave it to her closest friend to e-mail me. Her friend's message gave me only the barest outline of Kathy's story: a child dies, another is born twelve years later who has birthmarks matching the diseased body of the first child, and he remembers details about the life of the first child—was I interested in talking to her? I was definitely interested! I immediately e-mailed back with my phone number and urged Kathy to call. Then I waited. Sometimes I get teaser e-mails promising great cases, but the person on the other end gets cold feet and doesn't call. Fortunately, this wasn't one of those times. Kathy called a week later.

When I first talked to Kathy, I was drawn in by her down-to-earth, midwestern, deliberate way of speaking. With long and pensive pauses in her speech, she began her story, offering the "I hope you don't think I'm crazy" apologies that often open these first conversations. I promptly assured her that because I've heard every imaginable story about past lives and rebirth, *nothing* she could say would shock me.

As Kathy told her story, I could scarcely contain my excitement. She described the striking physical similarities between James's condition *at the time of his death*—which, therefore, could not be transmitted genetically—and the corresponding marks on newborn Chad. It wasn't just one place on his body that was affected by his past life, but four or five, and there was medical documentation to prove the correspondence. I had never seen such a strong physical case for reincarnation before. As a researcher, I understood the significance of what I was hearing and how valuable the case could be as evidence for reincarnation. No matter how remarkable a child's statements are, as in Peter's case in the previous chapter, or how specific and idiosyncratic the behaviors, as in Dylan's, there will always be some room for doubt. But such unmistakable *physical* evidence linking two lives, as I was hearing Kathy describe, cannot be easily explained away as coincidence or error.

As a mother, I was bowled over by the emotional and spiritual power of Kathy's unfolding drama. This was truly heart-wrenching stuff. And the way Kathy expressed herself was so genuine. Because she was straight from America's Bible Belt, was raised as a Baptist, had never read any books about reincarnation, and was unfamiliar with New Age concepts, her first-hand observations of this miracle were fresh and unsullied, her language wise and homespun. She spoke about reincarnation as if she had just discovered it on her own. And, in a way, she certainly had. Kathy was relieved to finally be able to talk freely about James and Chad with someone who didn't doubt her, and she hoped that I could give her some guidance, because, as she said, "Miracles are great, but they sure can be confusing."

For example, she asked, how does one comprehend rebirth—is it the same soul in a new body, or two souls in the same body, or something else? What is a soul and what does it mean for the soul to reincarnate? Kathy was tapping into the heart of the mystery. She struggled with this enigma as she noticed how the personality of James would sometimes come to the forefront in Chad: "Chad is basically a very quiet child, but when he speaks about James, he's full of excitement and energy. So to me, it's dealing with two personalities in one. I've known people with multiple personalities, but I am dealing with something else. I'm dealing with two children who are mine—Chad and James—in one body. It's mind-blowing."

These are questions that baffle theologians and philosophers. Yet Kathy was facing them every day. She was in the unique position not only to witness but also to *feel* the striking similarities between her two sons, one dead and one living. She was literally face-to-face with reincarnation. Questions about the nature of the soul were not an intellectual exercise for her, but were visceral, reverberating in every cell of her body.

I didn't have any pat answers for her. She was entering uncharted emotional and spiritual territory, traveling more deeply than anyone I had yet known, beyond where I had been with my own children. All I could do was be her confidante and share what I learned from other rebirth cases to give her a point of reference. I assured Kathy that from the cases I had already studied, reincarnation in the same family is indeed possible. In fact, from the many documented cases of it in the West and hundreds from other cultures and countries around the world, I'm convinced it is a universal and natural phenomenon. I told her about

Dr. Ian Stevenson's many fully documented cases, strikingly similar to Chad's case, that involved birthmarks and birth defects corresponding to marks on the deceased. So even that part wasn't a surprise.

Kathy needed no convincing that her son was back. That was clear. But it comforted her to learn that she and Chad were not alone. She eagerly absorbed everything I could tell her about other cases of children's past life memories, and it gave her a framework for understanding this new reality she and Chad were both experiencing.

## Past Life Healing

As Kathy felt more comfortable in sharing her insights and questions with me, she admitted that she believed Chad came back to her for a reason. She knew it wasn't a random coincidence. Now she wondered, what *was* the reason? Why did he return?

I told her that some of the cases I had studied suggest that there are, in fact, logical reasons why souls return to the same family: to be with those they love again, to continue learning and growing, and to heal both emotionally (as in Dylan's and Peter's cases) and physically. Yes, it is possible for children to heal *physical* symptoms that stem from past lives, after they have a chance to talk freely about their memories and gain closure on their former experiences.

As examples of how a physical problem from a past life can be healed, I shared two stories with Kathy. The first was about my own son Chase. When he was five, he developed a hysterical fear of loud booming sounds. Since infancy, he also had chronic eczema on his right wrist that did not respond to medical treatment. Shortly after his phobia first appeared, he shocked us with clear and emotional memories of being a black soldier killed in a Civil War battle. He recounted his vivid experience on the battlefield from the point of view of an adult, not a child. He explained how he had been scared and confused in the chaos of battle and sad because he missed his wife and children. He also described how he had been wounded in his right wrist (the same spot where Chase had the chronic eczema) and taken to a crude field hospital where he was treated and then ordered back into battle. A cannon shot finally killed him; he described his death, floating out of his body, and looking down on the smoky field below.

My son confessed that he still felt guilty about his role as a soldier who had to kill others to survive. I encouraged him to express his feelings and assured him that he was not to blame for his participation in battle even if he had to kill others—he was just doing his job at the time. I spoke to him on a soul level, explaining to him that in different lifetimes we play different roles, like actors in a play. By moving through different roles, we learn what it is to be human and how to be better people. Surprisingly, this simple explanation worked: Chase was visibly relieved. Then, within a few days, the eczema on his wrist cleared up completely, never to return. His phobia of loud booming sounds also completely disappeared, so much so that he has grown up to be an avid drummer. I found Chase's experience so extraordinary that, from that point on, researching children's past life memories became my passion.

The other story of healing was told to me by a mother from Connecticut who first approached me at one of my lectures in Virginia Beach. Patricia Austrian was convinced that her son Edward's potentially fatal tumor was healed when he remembered a past life. As a baby, Edward had always had trouble swallowing. When he learned to talk, he would point to his throat and complain, "My shot hurts, my shot hurts!" His parents assumed he was comparing the pain in his throat to getting a shot in the arm, which he hated. When he was three, however, his parents were alarmed to discover a large growth in his throat. A specialist told them he had a dangerous thyroglossal duct cyst that had to be removed as soon as possible. So they scheduled surgery. But the surgeon required Edward to have a tonsillectomy first before he could return a few weeks later for a second operation to remove the tumor.

After the tonsillectomy, little Edward informed his parents that he didn't need the second operation because the "shot" was gone. They assumed their son was still delirious from the anesthesia and the surgery, so they let him babble on.

Then his utterances became even stranger. He told them that *when he was big before*, he had been a soldier in France named Walter. He complained he was too young to fight, he was only eighteen—a strange comment for a four-year-old! He said he was constantly cold, hungry, and lonesome. One very rainy and cold day, he and the other soldiers were trudging through the mud when a bullet hit him from behind and lodged in his throat. Four-year-old Edward then gave what was, his physician father attested later, a clinically accurate description of dying from a bullet wound in the throat—grisly details that very few adults, let alone a four-year-old, would know. He repeated his story, word for word, over the next few days.

His parents were baffled by the realism of Edward's story. They couldn't figure out how he knew these things, especially his description of the death. They were amazed and shocked to discover that within three days the tumor had completely disappeared. Edward's surgeon was most surprised by this spontaneous remission of the tumor because he had never before heard of it happening with this type of tumor, and he fully expected it to return. Though, for more than ten years now, it hasn't.

After priming Kathy with these stories about the healing possibilities of past life memories, I asked her what the prognosis was for Chad's eye. She explained that since the specialists couldn't find any physiological cause for his blindness, they really didn't know how to fix it. Then she wondered out loud, "If there are some emotional issues that James and I need to resolve from the past, some unfinished business, and we can work through it, do you think it could heal Chad's eye?"

I told Kathy, "Yes, I believe it is possible."

## Now "Never" Has Come

Over the next few months, Kathy and I spent many hours on the phone discussing Chad and James and probing the possibilities of unfinished business from the past. All of this was stirring painful emotions in Kathy. But as difficult as it was, she was committed to healing her son and herself.

First we had to figure out what unfinished business

of James's needed to be addressed. We could only guess what his soul was expressing through Chad's physical symptoms and his desire to return to the old house. Was Chad hinting at something unfinished with his one comment, *"because I left you there"*? Could this be the clue to what he needed from Kathy? Did he come back simply because he had died too young and missed his mother and wanted to be with her again?

I told Kathy the story of Gary, who had died in the fire, and how apparently he had come back to be with his mother, Edith. This struck a chord with Kathy. "Perhaps James came back because of my desperate need, my selfish need, to have him back, as well as his own need to come back and continue his life since he died so young. Perhaps, in some way, my prayers drew him back to me." Although there is no way to know for sure what a soul needs, or why it returns, Kathy's reasons sounded plausible.

It was easier to determine what *Kathy's* unfinished business might be. She admitted she had never fully grieved for James or fully accepted his death. Because James had implored her not to cry for him, she hadn't. Instead she bottled up her grief. "I guess that somewhere in my mind I'm guilt-ridden because I did what I was asked to do, even though it wasn't what I wanted to do. Sometimes I wonder if James really needed me to cry for him so he would know how much I loved him."

Throughout this period, four-year-old Chad continued to talk about his life as James. For example, Kathy tells of the time he remembered his surgery. "The other night we were talking about his eye, and he asked me if he needed surgery again. I said, 'No, you've never had surgery.' He said, 'Yes I did, remember? It was over my ear.' I asked, 'What ear?' He pointed to his right ear. James had had a biopsy of the tumor over his right ear and Chad was born with a cyst on that very spot. I asked him if he knew why he had the surgery. He told me no. I asked him if it had hurt and he said, 'No, I was asleep.' "

It still surprised Kathy when Chad had fleeting memories that seemed to pop out of nowhere. I tried to persuade her that these moments were the openings she needed to help him resolve his unfinished business, that when he said these things, his past life memory was close to the surface. I told her she could use these openings to ask questions and try to figure out if there was anything still bothering Chad from his former life.

These were also opportune moments to tell Chad that she knew he was James reborn. This acknowledgment alone might open the door wider into this other reality where she could speak directly to James's soul—that part of him that still expressed itself through Chad. I suggested that while they were together in this space of mutual understanding, she could address James directly and tell him how she felt. She could say something like, "I was very sad when you died, but I know you had to leave your diseased body, and now I'm very happy to have you back."

I suggested that she also needed to assure him he was now in a healthy body and in a different lifetime. This is an important point. For, as bizarre as it sounds, other cases show that some souls do not comprehend that they have made the transition into a new body. In the first few years of life, some young children confuse the past with the present. Memories of their past lives are as vivid to them as a birthday party or vacation trip to the beach that happened last week or last month.

They still identify with the emotions and the body of their former life. By simply having a parent clarify this distinction between past and present and point out to them that they are now in a new body, their souls seem to understand. Some children "get it" immediately: There is a sudden light of recognition in their eyes, a glow on their face, and a palpable weight is lifted from them. I have dealt with cases in which the change was so fast and so complete, it seemed magical.

But Kathy wasn't quite ready for this direct approach. As simple as it sounded and as much as she wanted to heal the past, she admitted it was difficult for her to trust the process. She was afraid that if she were to confront the past with Chad, the outpouring of pain from her old wound would be unbearable for her and too shocking for him. She confided that every time Chad talked about James it caused the deep hurt and perplexity she had buried away many years ago to well up again. "Chad's memories are opening up a wound that I tried to close. His death was so painful and final I swore I'd never go back to that day; I wanted to close the door on that chapter of my life and never open it up for anyone. And now 'never' has come and for some reason that door is being unlocked."

I understood Kathy's reluctance to plunge into the pain and her need for gentleness and slow pacing. Yet I also knew how badly she wanted to resolve whatever might be holding Chad back. So I encouraged her to address Chad's remarks head-on and not put him off for too long. I was concerned that this window of remembering would not stay open much longer and the opportunity for natural healing might be lost. In most of the cases I've seen, children speak spontaneously of their past life memories for only a short time, usually between the ages of two and seven. These episodes of lucidity are often brief and appear to be random, occurring only when the spirit moves the child. After the age of seven, children either forget the memories entirely, often denying that they ever had them, or the memories are much more difficult to access as they become layered over by cultural conditioning and a natural shift in the child's focus to the outside world.

I assured Kathy that, from my experience, the process was mercifully gradual, unfolding over time, giving both child and parent a chance to integrate what was happening. Other parents have told me it seemed "guided." Fortunately, as Chad continued to talk about James, she found that this was true: It was a gentle and measured process that didn't overwhelm her. Chad opened up for a few moments at a time, just enough for her to release her built-up emotional pressure in small spurts rather than in one big explosion. This, she found, was bearable.

Sometimes, when *she* felt ready to talk about the past and tried to steer the conversation around to James, nothing happened. Either Chad resisted or the energy simply wasn't there and he couldn't access the memories. She began to wonder if Chad sensed her reluctance by the tension in her voice or the anxious look on her face and then gauged his responses for her benefit. "If he notices I'm getting upset, it's like a safety valve—he shuts off. For whatever reason, I don't know. But I'm so very grateful Chad is so tuned in to my feelings and my emotions that he doesn't rush into everything at once." These conversations were a dance they were both learning.

For example, one night Kathy brought out a picture of James. She had never shown any pictures of him to Chad or to anyone else in the family, and she wanted to see how Chad would react when he saw one for the first time. "When he saw James, the grin and the expression on his face were hard to explain. He had a shocked look on his face. His jaw dropped, his eyes got big, and he gasped for air.

"I asked him, 'What's wrong?'

"He said, 'I've been wishing for this picture. I want it because it's me.'

"I didn't respond. I didn't want to say 'yes, it is,' or 'no, it isn't.' I wanted to stay neutral and see where he would go. But then the moment passed. The energy was gone and nothing more came from Chad."

Another time, when they were eating dinner, quite spontaneously Chad said to his older brother, "I want to tell you something: When I was two years old I got so sick I couldn't keep 7UP down. Then I died and I came back. When I die again, I'll be back again." At that moment his father walked into the room and the spell was broken. Chad didn't say any more, but what he did say could not have been more direct and clear. Kathy added that it was true about the 7UP, and no one else knew about it.

Kathy began to trust her gut instincts—her intuition—about timing. She never pushed, but waited. "I get this incredible feeling when I sense that the time is right to speak to Chad about his memories. I feel it all through my body. That's when it works. I don't know what it is, but I'll go back to my gut and wait until I feel that energy. I can feel when it's coming."

## Read the Book Slowly

It had been about six months since the first time Kathy and I spoke on the phone, and she continued to call me with more or less regular updates. I looked forward to her calls because each time her fresh insights taught me something new about what it is like to live with a reincarnated child. At moments, when I could step outside myself and imagine what a stranger would think of our conversations, I realized how truly amazing they were. We were not talking about the mundane concerns of parenting: potty training, schools, play groups, or the funny things kids say. We were discussing the healing of souls. And neither of us could predict how this mystery would resolve—whether Chad's symptoms would heal and Kathy would finally find peace.

There were long periods, lasting sometimes weeks, when I didn't hear from Kathy. When she finally did call she would explain that either Chad hadn't said anything new, or the kids had been sick, or she was simply overwhelmed by day-to-day responsibilities. I learned to be patient and wait. Once, after a particularly long spell of silence, I received a call. Kathy was unusually excited.

She told me she had felt the timing and energy were finally right to speak directly to Chad about James. "One evening I sat Chad down on my lap and said, 'I don't know everything, but I know you were here before and you were a very sick little boy. Then you had to go away so you could come back in a healthy body.' Chad just sat and listened to me as I spoke. Then his eyebrows lifted, his face lit up, and he chirped, 'I know.' Then he ran off to play. That's all there was to it.

"Two days later he came running into the kitchen all excited. He closed his right eye and said, 'Isn't it cool, I can see you out of this eye!' (meaning his left eye). I corrected him and told him he couldn't see with that eye, but he insisted he could. To test him, I suggested we play a little game we had often played. I held up three fingers and asked him to count them. He counted correctly. I tried it again with one finger. Again he was correct. A few hours later I tried the game again, just to reassure myself that he could see. And to my amazement, he could! Oh, the light I saw in his eyes and the smile on his face from the excitement of being able to see. Because this child could not see before out of that eye. This is such a blessing! When you have a child who has walked through life for almost five years with no vision at all in his eye and now he sees a little bit, it's a big thing."

Kathy was surprised by this sudden breakthrough. She was amazed that her simple statements had any effect on Chad. "It's funny, but a part of me felt that even if I did talk to Chad and acknowledge that he was James, nothing would happen. I was afraid he just would not understand. Even though I hoped and prayed for healing, I *never* expected what I got. Boy, was I wrong!"

I was thrilled by Kathy's good news. I urged her to take Chad to his ophthalmologist to have his eye tested. The doctor determined there was only a very slight improvement in his left eye, barely measurable. Kathy was surprised the testing didn't reveal more change. But the fact that Chad's improvement was only slight didn't diminish her elation.

To Kathy, *any* improvement was tangible evidence that something was changing for the better and gave her hope for future improvement. She believed her words had penetrated Chad to the deepest level, and his soul was beginning to understand and heal. She was beginning to understand how all healing has to occur first in this deepest level of being. "I pray that both of our souls continue healing. My ultimate desire is for Chad's soul to be at peace. In order for that to happen, there has to be closure on the past for both of us. If he felt guilty about leaving me or needed to know how sad I was when he died, he now knows I'm okay and he's loved. Now we're ready to deal with whatever comes up next. It seems that healing the soul is like reading a book slowly: You finish one chapter at a time."

Throughout the following year, five-year-old Chad continued to speak of his life as James, always spontaneously and randomly, but gradually less and less often. Kathy knew now that when the memories surfaced they were a blessing and an opportunity for healing. She no longer dreaded them, but welcomed them, and she regretted that they were fading.

Kathy also noticed, as time went on, that she felt lighter. "I don't feel I'm carrying that heavy load of guilt anymore—all those 'what ifs' and 'what could have beens' from James's death. I'm at peace. This new feeling surprises me because I've been carrying around those heavy feelings for so many years. Suddenly I feel happy. It's such a new feeling that sometimes I don't know what to do with it."

Now an active six-year-old, Chad rarely speaks of his life as James. He is growing into a robust and healthy child. His skinny little boy's body is filling out. He runs out to play with the neighborhood kids and is losing his shyness. He can't wait to start school in the fall. Kathy sees that he is truly becoming 100 percent Chad. In moments, though, especially when she catches his reflection at a certain angle in the mirror or sees the birthmark scar on his neck, she is reminded that James is still with her too, and this comforts her. She is thankful that Chad is healthy and has the chance to grow up and know the joys of childhood that James never knew.

"I look back and remember I prayed before he died to have James back as a child in a healthy body and be given a second chance. I prayed for it every night. But if someone had told me when James was dying that I'd have him back as another child, I would have thought they were on drugs and had completely lost their minds. If they had told me that my prayers would be answered, I would have thought that I was asking for too much, for the impossible. But now I'm very much at peace with the fact that James is reborn. I accept James as being a part of Chad. And I accept that this is the answer to my prayers."

# Chapter 3

## Reincarnation and Biology

*It was an emotional meeting. He was so happy to see her, he was close to tears. He asked if she remembered him, her father. It was difficult for the seventeen-year-old girl to accept such words coming from a three-year-old boy. But Chanai eventually provided enough details of her earlier private life to convince her to accept him as her father reborn.*

Some people ask me how I know a story like Kathy's is true. How do I know it's really a case of reincarnation, and not something else? Were Chad's birthmarks merely a coincidence upon which Kathy built an elaborate illusion to satisfy her longing for her dead son? And was I just encouraging her with this fantasy?

For that matter, how do we know that any of these same-family cases are true? Can't they all be explained by heredity, coincidence, or a child repeating something he overheard? Or by wishful thinking: Parents wanting so desperately for a child or relative to return to them that they become convinced of reincarnation based on the slightest clues.

Yes, I suppose some families do mistakenly convince themselves that they are seeing reincarnation based on false clues. But I rarely see such cases because, I suspect, if the evidence is slim, the families keep their hunches to themselves. What I do see are many cases with evidence so striking the parents are moved to speak about it. In the best cases, the evidence is so compelling it defies any normal explanation other than reincarnation. Wishful thinking—a phrase I hear skeptics use most often as a blanket explanation for the phenomenon—doesn't come close to explaining the unmistakable evidence some families are seeing.

I am convinced that many of the cases that come to my attention *are* authentic cases of reincarnation. And many of these are cases of family return. In this chapter, I will show you why I am convinced the cases are real.

## Truth in Numbers

I've collected hundreds of cases since 1988 when I began investigating children's past life memories. They come to me from people from all walks of life, from all parts of the United States and Canada, and some from Europe. They come from people who have always believed in reincarnation, and also from people who clearly did not believe in reincarnation before it happened to them. The cases are everywhere. They come to me by e-mail, on the Forum on my Web site,[1] and from people I meet at my lectures, on airplanes, in the supermarket, or at gatherings of friends. Once people discover that I know something about children's past lives, they open up and confess their "family secret." I'm continually amazed at how often this happens, and how common these cases seem to be. And, since so many of them are same-family cases, their sheer number convinces me that same-family reincarnation is a much more common phenomenon than anyone suspects.

To be fair, not all of the stories I hear are obvious cases of reincarnation. Some are too sparse, without enough signs to help me decide one way or the other. The child makes one or two striking statements about "when I was big before" and nothing else. Or he shows an unexplainable behavior but makes no statements to link it to another lifetime. The child may be remembering a past life, or he may not.

But in other cases I see a whole constellation of statements, behaviors, and physical characteristics that, when considered together, point to a past life. I can usually spot the genuine cases after a few minutes of talking to the parent, because they fit the pattern I've learned to trust as signs of a past life memory. In fact, it's amazing how often I see the same types of things in case after case: the very young age when the child first speaks of the past life, the serious and matter-of-fact tone, statements with specific references to the past, as well as the behaviors and physical characteristics that are consistent with the life of the deceased. You will begin to get a feeling for these patterns as you read more of the stories in this book.

The large number of similar cases I see is not the only thing that points to a real phenomenon. It's also *how* the parents are convinced, often against their will.

Most of the people who seek me out have no prior belief in reincarnation. The idea that a relative could be reborn to their family is the furthest thing from their minds. Many are initially upset by what they are witnessing in their child because it rattles their belief that "we only live once" and flies in the face of their religious training.

Yet, these parents are convinced because they know for a fact what their toddler has been exposed to. They know what hushed family secrets, tragedies, and embarrassments the family never talks about—especially around the kids. So, when the baby begins talking about these things, the family pays attention. They know what traits—a characteristic limp resulting from an injury, for example—could not be hereditary. Some notice birthmarks on the child that correspond to wounds or scars on the deceased. Even then, they resist calling it reincarnation and hunt for any rational explanation they can find, no matter how remote. Only after they have eliminated all normal explanations do they come to the conclusion that they are truly witnessing reincarnation in their own family.

Some parents who contact me are confused and want help understanding what is happening with their child. Even if they have no problem with reincarnation in theory, they struggle with the idea that a soul can return from the afterlife so soon. Or they've never heard of a soul returning to the same family and are afraid to think that their family is the bizarre exception. They feel alone and isolated. They also worry that something might be wrong with their child. So they are greatly relieved when I tell them they are *not* alone, that *many* other families are seeing the same thing in their children, and their child is not abnormal in any way. If anything, these children tend to be early talkers and, as they get older, are unusually articulate and aware.

Other parents need no convincing. By the time I talk to them they've been living with their reincarnated child for a while and have gotten used to it. As a device to test their conviction and learn what makes them so sure, I challenge these confident parents by suggesting explanations other than reincarnation. They answer by listing the telltale signs I've come to trust. Then, after we talk for a while and they grow more comfortable sharing their secrets with me, they describe the *feeling* they have for the child, the extraordinary bond they share, the deep connection that makes that child special. I've heard this so many times, I've come to believe that a profound, ineffable *knowing* is just as real as the more objective signs.

Almost all of the parents, once they have accepted that they are seeing reincarnation in their family, are hungry to explore its meaning and implications, to penetrate what it means to have a loved one return to them after death. They pour their hearts out to me and we explore together. The mystery is so deep and never-ending, I learn something new every time.

## Dr. Ian Stevenson

The cases I see every day have convinced me that same-family reincarnation is real. But few people have the opportunity to work as closely with these cases as I do. I understand it's hard for many people to change their minds on such a life-changing idea as reincarnation without experiencing it directly or seeing empirical evidence.

Fortunately, that kind of evidence exists. When a truly skeptical person challenges me on the truth of reincarnation and family return, I don't argue. Instead, to answer their need for hard evidence, I tell them about the work of Dr. Ian Stevenson of the University of Virginia, list his impeccable credentials, and describe his rigorous methods. Dr. Stevenson has conducted scientific research for the last forty years on children's spontaneous past life memories and amassed more than 2,600 cases. His work is so solid and respectable, it gives levelheaded Westerners permission to treat reincarnation as a serious subject, even to accept it as true, without compromising their trust in reason or science.

And, taking it a step further, his work gives Westerners permission to believe in *same-family* reincarnation as well. Same-family reincarnation is difficult to prove directly because it would require documenting things only the family can know for sure. But thanks to Dr. Stevenson, that's not a problem. He proves the general case: Children can and do remember recent past lives. So it follows that if some children can remember being a distant stranger in a past life, they can just as easily remember being a deceased relative. His bedrock evidence is the foundation for the credibility of my work in same-family reincarnation.

Ian Stevenson, M.D., is a doctor of psychiatry, a veteran of the scientific community with hundreds of academic articles and more than a dozen books to his credit. At the height of his career in conventional medicine, he was the head of the department of psychiatry at the University of Virginia. Now he is best known as a pioneer in reincarnation research. He has spent most of his sixty-year career (Stevenson is now in his eighties) perfecting methods for verifying the past life memories of children. He has compiled nearly a thousand cases in which the child made enough detailed and specific statements about his or her previous life that the deceased could be positively identified. Then, based on information from the child, Dr. Stevenson located the deceased's family and friends and verified the child's statements, behaviors, and physical characteristics by comparing them with the facts of the deceased person's life. In all of these nearly one thousand cases, he found a direct correspondence between the young child's memories and the life of the deceased.

Most of Dr. Stevenson's cases are not same-family cases. Because his main interest is in gathering evidence that will stand up to critical examination by the scientific community, he favors cases where he can show there was no contact between the families of the child and the deceased. This makes it easier to prove that the child is not simply repeating things he overheard. Still, Dr. Stevenson has found that same-family cases are common and he has hundreds in his files and published works.

The majority of Dr. Stevenson's cases are from Asian countries—India, Sri Lanka, Thailand, Lebanon, Turkey, Myanmar (formerly Burma)—as well as West Africa and tribes of the Pacific Northwest. At first glance it appears that the cases could be attributed to the fact that people in these countries believe in reincarnation—a cultural variation on the wishful-thinking idea. But for many reasons this is not true. First, there is no such thing as a universal belief in reincarnation, even in a country like India. The cases appear there both in families who believe and in those who don't believe. And if you read enough cases, you see that the parents in non-Western cultures have just as many reasons to resist reincarnation as an explanation for their child's strange behavior as Westerners do, though they are not always the same reasons.

Dr. Stevenson returns often to these countries for his research simply because it is easier to find cases there. The people in these cultures are familiar with reincarnation and not afraid to talk about it, so more cases rise to the surface and come to the attention of his well-established network of informants. This is in contrast to the West where we have a cultural taboo against taking reincarnation seriously and talking about it publicly. Because of the attitudes here, he finds it difficult to find good cases to investigate in the West, (but this is changing rapidly).

## Suleyman and the Flour Shovel

The story of Suleyman Capar is a typical Stevenson case. Unlike most of the American cases I've seen, the children in Dr. Stevenson's best cases have extremely clear memories of their past lives and a strong identification with the past life person they remember being. If this is the first time you've seen a story like this, its intensity may strike you as incredibly bizarre, like a fairy tale or allegory, and you may find it difficult to relate to as anything that can happen to a real child. But if you read more of Dr. Stevenson's cases, you will understand that these kinds of things really do happen, in rare instances, to real children. (I want to emphasize that Dr. Stevenson's cases represent the most extreme instances of children's past life memories. None of the American cases I've seen are as detailed as this.)

Dr. Stevenson's published version of Suleyman's case is a fourteen-page academic report full of abstruse commentary and tabulated detail. I've distilled the essence of the story here to highlight its most important features.[2]

Suleyman Capar was born in 1966 in a town on the Mediterranean coast of Turkey. As soon as he could put words together, he pointed away from his house and implored his parents to take him "to the stream." From then on he constantly begged to be taken "to the stream, to the stream!" As his ability with language improved, his past life story emerged in greater and greater detail. He said he was a miller named Mehmet from the village of Ekbar, and he was killed in a quarrel. Speaking in the present tense, he insisted, "I am married, I have two sons and a daughter, I have a horse." He remembered his mother and said his father had taken a second wife, adding, "I suppose the new wife has spent all the money."

He described his death. He was killed by an angry customer, also named Mehmet, who hit him on the head with a flour shovel. Little Suleyman repeated these facts until finally, when he was barely two years old, his mother took him to Ekbar, several villages away. Suleyman led her to the stream, the mill, and pointed out the house where he had lived. On a second visit he spontaneously recognized and greeted the mother of Mehmet Bekler. She admitted that her son had been a miller and was killed with a flour shovel in a quarrel four years earlier. Court records confirmed Suleyman's description of the murder. He was right about the family details too, including the fact that his father had taken a second wife (though he was wrong about the horse—the horse belonged to Mehmet's father).

The two families were not acquainted before all this happened—Suleyman's family ground their grain at a mill in their own village. As Suleyman grew up, he and Mehmet Bekler's family exchanged frequent visits, and he continued to believe he was Mehmet, even to the point of trying to claim Mehmet's land. On one visit to Ekbar he pointed at a strange man and angrily shouted, "He killed me!" The man was Mehmet Bayrakdar, the convicted murderer of Mehmet Bekler.

This story is typical of Dr. Stevenson's cases in a number of ways. Suleyman was very young, a baby just beginning to talk, when he first spoke of his past life. He made specific statements and gave proper names that enabled his mother to find his former family. He recognized Mehmet's mother, his murderer, and other individuals important in his previous life, all of which strengthened the credibility of his statements. Suleyman exhibited behaviors—his identification with the family and hatred for the murderer—that were perfectly appropriate to Mehmet's life. And he remembered his death. In a high percentage of Dr. Stevenson's cases, children vividly recall their most recent deaths.

## Reincarnation and Biology

There is one more important feature of Suleyman's case that I haven't mentioned yet. He had a birth defect, a physical link between his past and present life, that reinforces all the other evidence pointing to him as

Mehmet Bekler reborn. Birthmarks are common in many of Dr. Stevenson's cases and are prominent in all his recent work.

Three witnesses who were present at Suleyman's birth reported that the back of his skull was flattened and soft, the skin puckered and discolored like a scar. Dr. Stevenson himself inspected Suleyman when the boy was seven years old and reported that the birthmark was still prominent, soft and depressed, discolored, and had little hair growing on it. It looked very much like a badly healed wound from a blow to the back of the head. Checking Mehmet Bekler's postmortem report obtained from a government hospital, Dr. Stevenson confirmed that Suleyman's deformity matched the type, location, and size of the fatal wound from the flour shovel.

Can Suleyman's birth defect be explained away as a coincidence? Maybe, if his were the only case like this, it could be passed over as an unexplainable curiosity. But it's not. It is one of 225 cases featuring birthmarks or birth defects published in 1997 in Dr. Stevenson's book *Reincarnation and Biology: A Contribution to the Etiology of Birthmarks and Birth Defects*. Almost all of these cases document a child who has birthmarks or birth defects that correspond closely to a mark or injury, usually a fatal injury, on the deceased person he or she remembers being. In most, the child makes enough statements and recognitions to enable Dr. Stevenson to identify the deceased person and verify that the birthmarks and birth defects do indeed match wounds on the body of the deceased.

The book is a massive accomplishment—literally. Its two volumes contain 2,268 pages and weigh eight pounds. Leafing through it, you can see it is full of charts, anatomical diagrams, autopsy photographs, X rays, detailed case descriptions, technical footnotes, numerous appendices, and Dr. Stevenson's extensive analysis and comments throughout. It's a no-nonsense academic work intended for the medical community.

*Reincarnation and Biology* is revolutionary not only for its scope and size, but also because it raises the standard of evidence in the reincarnation debate. It gives tangible evidence that a newborn's body can bear the imprint of a past life. The birthmarks and birth defects can be observed and photographed; in some cases Dr. Stevenson was able to compare them to autopsy reports and hospital records. In the best cases, the odds are so astronomically high against random chance that they are comparable to the statistical standards accepted in conventional medical research.

The birthmarks featured in *Reincarnation and Biology* are not the common moles that everyone has. Most are the rarest kind of birthmark, consisting of either puckered or depressed tissue, often colorless and hairless. In other words, they look like scars. In addition, some of the children have two or more birthmarks or birth defects that match two or more wounds and scars—the record for one case is eight matches[3]—further multiplying the odds against random coincidence. The birthmarks that I think argue most dramatically against coincidence are the double birthmarks from gunshot wounds. Dr. Stevenson includes fourteen cases where the child's body shows a small, round birthmark that matches exactly the size, shape, and location of the entrance wound of a bullet that killed the person the child remembers being. On the opposite side of the child's body in each case is a larger, irregular birthmark that corresponds to the wound where bullet and bone fragments tore a larger, irregular hole while exiting the other side of the victim's body.[4]

And that's only the birthmarks. Of this two-volume work, one is devoted entirely to birth defects. The birth *defects* in these cases are more rare than the scarlike birthmarks. They include missing limbs, fingers, and other gross distortions of the body, illustrated throughout the volume with clinical photographs.

For example, one particularly striking photo in the birth-defects volume is that of a little Burmese girl born with her right leg missing just below the knee. She remembered the life of a young, desperately poor teenage girl who survived by selling roses to passengers at the village railroad station. She was run over by a train, killing her and severing her right leg. As in most of the cases in *Reincarnation and Biology*, the child made detailed statements and a number of recognitions that convinced the family she was the reincarnation of the teenager who was killed by the train. She also had a marked phobia of trains. Dr. Stevenson takes care to show with medical citations how rare and unusual her birth defect is.[5]

A little boy from India had another rare deformity. He was born missing all the fingers on his right hand. The photograph shows that the deformed fingers end at the same point, as if they were all cut in a single stroke. His other hand and the rest of his body are normal. He remembered the life of a young boy who lost the fingers on his right hand when he accidentally inserted it into a fodder-chopping machine, a device with large, unguarded rotating blades. Again, Dr. Stevenson analyzes and discusses the rarity of the deformity and illustrates his analysis with an X ray showing the bone structure of both the boy's hands.[6]

## Chanai Choomalaiwong Inquires About His Jeans

The cases I've described to this point are mere summaries of the accounts published in *Reincarnation and Biology*. They don't do justice to the level of detail in a typical Stevenson case. To give you a feeling for how complete some of the stories are, here is one of my favorites—the story of Chanai. It shows how statements, behaviors, and birthmarks combine to make powerful evidence for reincarnation. Beyond the proof issue, this narrative hints at the human drama lying beneath Dr. Stevenson's academic reports.

A notable feature of Chanai's case is the *double* birthmark that neatly corresponds to the fatal entry and exit wounds from Chanai's previous life. It is also an example of how, as in most of these cases, the statements emerge *before* the family knows anything about the deceased, countering the criticism that the family fabricated the statements to retroactively explain the birthmarks.[7]

> Chanai Choomalaiwong was born in rural Thailand in 1967. Soon after his birth, his parents, who were very poor, went in different directions to find work, leaving Chanai in the care of his grandmother, Prom. Prom raised ducks for a living.
>
> When Chanai was three years old, Prom noticed that whenever he played with other children, he would pretend to be a schoolteacher. He took his role seriously and ordered his playmates to bring him paper for their school.
>
> Around this time he also told his grandmother that he had been a schoolteacher named Bua Kai in his last life, and he had been shot in the back of the head and

killed on his way to school. He added that his parents
were Kian and Yong, and he had a wife named Suan
and twin daughters, Toi and Tim. He told his grandmother that if she took him to a town called Ban Khao
Phra, he would show her where he had lived and she
could meet his family. Prom did not agree to this,
though, for she was skeptical that her grandson was
actually remembering a previous life. And she was
worried that if they approached strangers with his
claim that he was their relative reborn and proved to
be wrong, she would look foolish indeed.

The three-year-old became fixated on the idea of
finding his family, and he wouldn't leave his grandmother alone; he constantly cried and begged to go to
Ban Khao Phra. Tired of his pestering, Prom threat-
ened to punish him if he mentioned it again. But he
persisted in spite of her threats. Finally, Prom gave in.
She took Chanai by bus to the town closest to Ban
Khao Phra, which was thirty kilometers away.

When they got off the bus in the marketplace, three-
year-old Chanai led his grandmother down a dirt road
directly to a house. There they were greeted by an elderly couple named Kian and Yong—just as Chanai
had predicted. The child promptly introduced himself
to the couple as Bua Kai, and addressed them as
"Mother" and "Father." The couple must have been
shocked by this presumptuous child appearing at their
door claiming to be their son—who in fact had been
murdered some eight years before. However, they
were sufficiently intrigued by this startling introduc-
tion to invite Prom and Chanai into their home. They
listened in disbelief as the child recounted his memories of being a schoolteacher who had twin daughters
and was shot in the back of the head while on his way

to school. But it wasn't until they saw that Chanai had two birthmarks on his head—one small round one in the back and a larger irregular one on the left side of his forehead—that they took his claim seriously. They promptly invited Chanai and his grandmother to visit again soon.

When they returned a few days later, other curious members of the Kai family gathered to meet them. They immediately began to test Chanai's memory. Someone pointed to a woman in the group and asked who she was. Without hesitating, Chanai said, "It is Suan, of course." Suan was Bua Kai's widow. They asked him to recount the events from the day Bua was killed. Chanai gave a detailed description of Bua's last day—how he had done his laundry, taken a shower, and had placed a Buddha necklace on a table before he bicycled to school. He remarked that Bua had forgotten to put on his necklace and had not taken his pistol with him, and that they both would have been stolen by the murderers if he had done so. The relatives, trying to confuse him and test his memory, insisted he had been shot coming *home* from school. Chanai didn't fall for this, and repeated that he had been on his way *to* school. They asked him to describe the necklace. He said it had Buddhas on it and held up three fingers to indicate how many. They produced the actual necklace, which had only one amulet on it. Seeing the necklace angered Chanai, and he asked where the other Buddhas were. The family admitted they had given two amulets to Bua's sons after his death.

Everything else Chanai said was accurate too. As a final test, Bua's mother brought out six gun cartridge belts and told Chanai that if he could pick the one that had belonged to Bua, she would accept him as her son reborn. Prom sat there anxiously, as the pressure was on her grandson with this final test—her reputation was at stake as well. Without hesitating, Chanai picked a belt with three cartridges in it and said, "Mother, this is my belt." He was right. Bua's family was moved to tears; they were now convinced that Chanai was Bua Kai reborn.

Everything Chanai said was correct. Bua Kai had been a schoolteacher who had a wife, Suan, two sons, and twin daughters, Tim and Toi. While bicycling to school one day, he was shot in the head from behind; the bullet exited his forehead above the left eye. Dr. Stevenson reports that, aside from being a family man and schoolteacher, Bua Kai had a darker side. He was flirtatious with women and was rumored to have had extramarital affairs. He was also involved with local gangsters and owned several guns. Either of these activities could have supplied the motive for his murder. There was a police inquiry into the murder, but because of a lack of evidence, no arrests were made.

After Chanai was accepted by the Kai family as Bua reborn, he fell completely into the role of Bua Kai. He became possessive toward Bua's belongings and his former children. For example, he went around the house and remarked on missing pieces of furniture and books that the family had removed after Bua's death. He asked about a small medical bag Bua used as a first-aid kit at his school, and then on his own he went upstairs and found it in a room. He asked about a pair of jeans Bua had purchased shortly before his death but had never worn. When Suan, his widow, admitted she had used them for herself, Chanai grumbled and muttered something about her always using his things for herself.

Chanai was reunited with Bua's twin daughters, meeting Tim first. It was an emotional meeting. He was so very happy to see her, he was close to tears. He asked if she remembered him, her father. It was difficult for the seventeen-year-old girl to accept such words coming from a three-year-old boy. But Chanai provided enough details of her earlier private life to convince her to accept him as her father reborn. Chanai asked to see her sister Toi. When he finally met her, he asked her if she was still very sensitive. Because of the uncomfortable age difference between Chanai and the girls, and the awkwardness of the situation, they initially addressed him as *little nephew*. Chanai refused to accept this. He told them he would not talk to them again unless they addressed him properly as *Father*. They reluctantly gave in to this bizarre demand. One of their brothers, however, would not do so, and Chanai shunned him.

Chanai visited the family of Bua Kai often, sometimes accompanied by his grandmother Prom. He always brought pieces of sugarcane as gifts for the girls, which was what Bua had always done. When he was not yet four years old, he would occasionally sneak off to the bus without informing his grandmother and would tell the driver to leave him off at the other village. Prom, upon finding him missing, always knew where he had gone and would have to go fetch him. The attachment between Chanai and Bua Kai's family became so strong that the Kais proposed adopting him. Prom, however, would not give up this child she loved so dearly.

## The Mind/Body Question

In the face of overwhelming evidence in a case like Chanai's, some people who still hold to the idea that reincarnation is not possible try to dismiss the evidence by attacking Dr. Stevenson's methods. They presume he must have made mistakes, or the families were in cahoots and tricked him into believing their hoax. Or they question Stevenson's own objectivity, guessing that a man so dedicated to proving reincarnation must be tainting his evidence.

With so much riding on the credibility of one man, how well do his methods and objectivity hold up under closer scrutiny?

They hold up very well. In fact, the more one knows about Dr. Stevenson, the *more* convincing the evidence becomes, not less. The man himself emerges as a fascinating character, something of an iconoclast, a fiercely independent thinker unafraid to challenge entrenched opinions if he doesn't believe they are supported by objective evidence. "For me everything now believed by scientists is open to question, and I am always dismayed to find that many scientists accept current knowledge as forever fixed. They confuse the product with the process."[8]

Dr. Stevenson never set out to prove reincarnation. He is, first and foremost, a medical researcher, and his primary goal has always been to better understand the origins of disease and personality. But his approach is fundamentally different from that of other medical researchers. He bases his theories on the idea that the mind, as an entity *separate* from the body, can influence the biochemistry of disease and personality. This is a radical idea now, and was even more radical in the

1940s, when he began his career. Most scientists in the twentieth century based their work on the premise that the body is a machine, the sum of its biochemical parts, and that the mind is the product of the tissues of the brain. Dr. Stevenson, inspired by his extensive reading in fields outside medicine, has always rejected this premise as overly narrow and not supported by the facts.

He began his career in the new field of psychosomatic medicine, studying the effects of emotion on disease. Even as a young doctor he made major contributions to the field. Then he studied Freudian psychoanalysis hoping it would shed light on how the subconscious mind influences disease and behavior. But he quickly became disenchanted with Freud's theories because they were, in his estimation, unscientific and ill-reasoned, with little basis in objective research. He criticized Freud as an emperor without clothes—a brave statement at the time when Freud's ideas dominated psychiatry and psychology.

In the early 1950s, Dr. Stevenson began to concentrate on the question "What survives bodily death?" as a means to demonstrate that the mind can function independently of the body. This led him to explore paranormal phenomena—apparitions and disembodied spirits, death visions, near-death experiences, and mediums. It didn't bother him that the medical establishment rejected the paranormal as an unfit topic for responsible research and a poor career choice.

As he began to design experiments to gather objective evidence supporting the existence of paranormal phenomena, he ran into a major problem. He discovered how difficult it is to separate the evidence for the phenomena from the expectations, prior knowledge, and bias of his subjects, who were all adults. Then, in 1960, he made a breakthrough. He discovered in his readings a scattering of cases of children's past life memories and realized that very young children would make ideal research subjects because it is possible to know what a young child has been exposed to. He threw himself into the systematic study of children's past life memories to answer the question "What survives bodily death?" Now, after forty years of collecting and publishing cases, he is considered to be the father of reincarnation research, with scientists around the world adopting his methods and duplicating his results.

Many people credit Dr. Stevenson with providing empirical evidence for reincarnation, but, ironically, he is not eager to take the credit. He would much rather talk about the contribution his work, especially *Reincarnation and Biology: A Contribution to the Etiology of Birthmarks and Birth Defects*, makes to medical science (*etiology* is the medical term for "origin of a disease"). Scientists have no explanation for what causes more than two-thirds of all birthmarks and birth defects. Dr. Stevenson offers a theory that has evidence to back it up: Some are caused by injuries sustained in a past life. In a way, his career has come full circle. "These cases have brought me back to my principal interest in medicine: psychosomatic relationships. However, now we are talking about a mind's influence on a body across the gap of death."

## How to Prove a Past Life Memory

What are the chances that Dr. Stevenson makes mistakes when he's in the field collecting data? Is there some underlying flaw in his method that would allow an explanation other than reincarnation for his thousands of cases?

I've discovered that most of the people who try to poke holes in Dr. Stevenson's evidence by criticizing his field methods have not taken the time to understand all he does when he documents his cases. They have no conception of how systematic and thorough his investigations really are. The heart of his method is the interview, and Dr. Stevenson is an expert in this area. Early in his career he wrote a clinical textbook for psychiatrists, *The Diagnostic Interview,* based on methods lawyers use to reconstruct past events for presentation as evidence in a court of law. Multiple interviews are the key. He'll interview many witnesses separately and compare the results. He'll return to reinterview key witnesses months, even years, later to see how well their testimony holds up. Under such close scrutiny from a professional interviewer, it is inconceivable that anyone, especially unsophisticated third-world villagers, could conceal a hoax, or pass off their exaggerations and fantasies as fact.

When Dr. Stevenson begins to probe a case, he always visits the child and the family at their home—they never come to him. He interviews the child and anyone close to the child. He documents and cross-checks any statements or behaviors the child made before the case was widely known. For example, if one of the first things the child said was that he owned two horses in his past life, Stevenson will try to find two or more people who witnessed the young child saying he owned two horses in his past life.

If the case shows promise, it will contain enough information to identify the deceased person the child remembers being (termed the *previous personality* in his writings). Dr. Stevenson will make a surprise visit to the village of the previous personality and conduct a whole new series of intensive interviews. He will record everything he can find about the life of the previous personality and the circumstances of his or her death, and then compare it with the child's statements and behaviors. Using the example of the horses, he will look for witnesses to verify that the deceased did in fact own two horses. (If the deceased owned only one horse, or if the two horses were actually owned by a brother, Stevenson will dutifully mention the discrepancy in his write-up.) If a birthmark is involved, he takes pictures of the marks or deformities on the child, then attempts to locate court records and autopsy or medical reports of the deceased.

As he proceeds with the fact gathering, Dr. Stevenson diligently pursues all explanations other than reincarnation for what the child said and did. He considers normal ways the child might have learned about the deceased, including the most improbable scenarios for overhearing adult conversations. He's alert for hoaxes, self-deception, or exaggeration by the families. He considers genetic memory, though in most cases inherited transfer is clearly impossible—for example, when a child remembers details of his own murder. If he finds a plausible, normal explanation for the memories, he drops the case and moves on.

Dr. Stevenson explores the possibility of ESP and spirit possession. In most of the cases, ESP cannot explain the memories, let alone the behaviors and birthmarks. It would take a psychic of the most extraordinary ability and sophistication to get all of the facts and recognitions correct. Think of the number of details in

Chanai's case, for example. Yet most of these children show no psychic ability. Also, for many reasons that he explains in his books, the cases do not fit the pattern of spirit possession.

In the best cases, the only remaining possibility is reincarnation, and these he writes up and publishes. In each of his write-ups he lays out every detail of the process and invites the reader to evaluate his methods as well as the results. He highlights all possible problems with each case and discusses how the memories might be explained normally, no matter how remote or preposterous the "normal" explanation is. This abundance of detail and fastidious discussion is why his books are a chore to read and one of the reasons his work is not more widely known.

Dr. Stevenson, true to his scholarly character, will never go so far as to say he has proven reincarnation. As he has insisted repeatedly in interviews, he's not trying to prove anything. His goal is to provide the highest-quality, most objective evidence possible. He invites us to draw our own conclusions.

## Making Reincarnation Real

When we are satisfied that the cases in *Reincarnation and Biology* are true, and when we can put the question of proof behind us, a couple of interesting things happen.

First, the burden of proof for reincarnation is lifted from individual families. Families with young children who show signs of a past life memory do not have to prove reincarnation to anybody. It is possible. It happens all the time. Yes, they should assess the evidence and decide for themselves if it's true in their case or not. But they can decide according to their own standards, not anyone else's, and trust their eyes and ears and hearts. Instead of fretting about proof, they can focus on how best to respond to the child so the child gets the most benefit, and open themselves to the lessons the child brings for their own lives.

For the rest of us, it isn't necessary to scrutinize each and every past life story we hear, including all the same-family cases in this book, as a self-contained proof of reincarnation. We can move beyond asking of each case, "Can it be? Is it possible?" and instead look for the patterns, lessons, and nuances of meaning.

We can begin looking to this phenomenon for answers to age-old metaphysical questions. In each of his verified cases, Dr. Stevenson documents both sides of the reincarnational equation—the life of the deceased and of the reincarnated child—giving us a unique opportunity to compare two incarnations of the same soul and observe what carries over from life to life. We can move beyond the fuzzy religious concept of "soul" and talk more precisely about the kinds of memories, behavior, personality, talents, feelings, relationships, and even physical characteristics that survive the journey from death to rebirth.

We can open ourselves to the stories for new insights into our own lives. I find that reading past life cases inspires introspection in the same way reading a good novel, biography, or memoir does. The cases may read like fiction, with bizarre plot twists more wildly original than most science-fiction novels or fantasy movies—wrenching murders narrated by the *victims*, quarrels and loving reunions that span death and rebirth, and children who yearn for their "other mother" and sometimes find themselves with *two* families to love them.

The cases read like fiction, but now we know they are not. They describe the lives of real people—real fathers, mothers, grandparents, and children. The stories are full of the drama of relationships, emotions, struggles, and ambitions with all of the color and shading we recognize from our own lives. When you accept the stories as true, they bring reincarnation down to earth, out of the realm of spiritual abstraction. They make reincarnation human.

Indeed, past life cases add a new dimension to the human drama. They broaden our concept of what human is: human spans lifetimes.

# Chapter 4

## Chicago, USA

*The two doctors leaned over little Chad, moving him into the slanting yellow rays of the afternoon sun. They nodded confirmingly to each other as they gently examined his neck. Dr. Stevenson pointed to a distinct scarlike birthmark. Even to my untrained eye, it didn't look like any mole or discolored birthmark I had ever seen. It looked like a surgical scar. This was a big moment for me: I had been reading about these rare birthmarks in Dr. Stevenson's works for years. Here was a striking example in the flesh.*

Much to everyone's relief, as the calendar turned to January 1, 2000, no planes fell from the sky due to Y2K computer glitches. So in the second week of the new millennium, I went ahead with my plans to join Dr. Stevenson and his colleague, Dr. Jim Tucker, on a field investigation of two of my cases in the Chicago area, including Chad Luke's case.

This trip to Chicago would be my third visit with Dr.

Stevenson. I was excited to be asked along because the trip might very well be the last field investigation of his long career because he will be retiring this year. I was sad to hear this; I've gotten to know Dr. Stevenson only in the last few years. But I was happy to learn that "retirement" for Dr. Stevenson means he'll be finishing several books in progress, including a book on American reincarnation cases.

Jim Tucker, a child psychiatrist from Charlottesville, will be continuing Dr. Stevenson's research at the University of Virginia. Jim and I share a marvelously synchronistic connection. When I lived in Asheville, North Carolina, many years ago, I had a dear friend, Chris. We used to have wonderful, deep discussions about soul mates and the meaning of love and fate while we kept an eye on our young children splashing in the community swimming pool. This was before either of us knew there was such a thing as children's past life memories. As happens in the ebb and flow of friendships, Chris moved away and we lost touch. The last thing I heard was that she was working toward her doctorate in psychology somewhere in Virginia. Soon after *Children's Past Lives* was published, I got an e-mail from Jim, who introduced himself as Dr. Stevenson's research colleague—and Chris's new husband!

This trip to Chicago was special for another reason: I would finally meet Kathy Luke. Although we had developed a close relationship through dozens of intense phone conversations over the past two and a half years, we had never met face-to-face. And, of course, I was curious to meet Chad and the other family members I had heard so much about and to see Chad's birthmarks for myself.

It was arranged that the two psychiatrists and I would rendezvous at the rental-car terminal at enormous O'Hare Airport. I was delighted to see both of them arrive. Dr. Stevenson—tall, thin, and silver-haired—walked in lugging a road-worn suitcase bound with a strap. I wondered how many miles and how many countries that suitcase had traveled. Jim, forty years his junior, is also tall, a handsome man with a beautiful glow about him. As we headed out of the building, I was quickly reminded that Dr. Stevenson, the consummate gentleman, practices the all but extinct courtesy of opening doors for women.

We started off with the two tall men squeezed into the front seats of our compact rental car. I, with the shortest legs, sat in the back. I had a million pent-up questions in my mind, but I tried to contain myself, at least until they navigated through the tangle of highways around the airport and we were well on our way speeding up the straight interstate to northern Illinois. Then I reminded myself I had three days to ask my questions, so I relaxed and let myself get into the rhythm of the trip.

## In the Flesh

This was Dr. Stevenson and Jim's second visit to the Luke home. I had brought Chad's case to their attention in late 1997 because I knew they would be interested in his distinct multiple birthmarks, particularly since they were supported by medical documentation. On that first trip, they had interviewed Kathy and Chad as well as other family members and witnesses, examined Chad's neck and body, and obtained James's medical records. Jim told me it was perhaps the strongest birthmarks case Dr. Stevenson had seen in the United States. They were so impressed by the case, they wrote it up and submitted it to several medical journals. This was their follow-up visit. As is his policy with cases in other parts of the world, Dr. Stevenson was revisiting Chad Luke, now seven years old, to reconfirm the facts of the case and check on his progress.

Jim recognized the Luke house among the many others just like it sitting squarely in a neat row on a tree-lined street in this small midwestern city. Kathy greeted us at the door and led us into a dark living room dominated by a large-screen TV glowing in the corner. Perched next to the TV, a caged cockatiel eyed us suspiciously as we entered.

Kathy and I shook hands and looked deeply into each other's eyes, matching voices to faces. She is a tall, thin woman with long brown hair and penetrating eyes. Kathy's husband, Billy, was there along with her three other children. When I asked where Chad was, Kathy said he was acting shy and hiding in his room. Eventually she coaxed him out to join us.

Dr. Stevenson led us into the discussion with his amicable, yet straightforward line of questioning. Jim joined in too. They asked Kathy and Billy about Chad's development since their last visit and reviewed the facts of the case. I listened intently, noting Dr. Stevenson's interviewing techniques while, at the same time, Chad and I scoped each other out as he played on the floor at my feet. When he glanced up at me from his play, I could see his opaque eye and the slight distortion on the left side of his face that Kathy had often mentioned. His shyness dissolved when I presented him with a gift from my bag— a Beanie Baby walrus. We were best friends after that.

On the surface, the scene looked like any casual living-room visit. But a lot was going on. I was observing Chad, talking to Chad's father, and listening to the two psychiatrists question Kathy, all at the same time. At one point Dr. Stevenson asked Chad to walk across the room. The last time they had examined him, the limp in his left leg—the one that had been tumor-ridden and fractured on James—was clearly noticeable. Now there was only the slightest hint of irregularity in his stride, but I could see it was still there. Then Dr. Stevenson asked Chad if he could look at his neck. He and Jim leaned over the little boy, moving him into the slanting yellow rays of the afternoon sun streaming through the window blinds. The two doctors nodded confirmingly to each other as they gently examined his neck. Dr. Stevenson invited me over to have a look. He pointed to a distinct scarlike mark on the side of Chad's neck. Even to my untrained eye, it didn't look like any mole or discolored birthmark I had ever seen. It looked like a surgical scar. This was a big moment for me: I had been reading about these rare birthmarks in Dr. Stevenson's works for years, and here was a striking example in the flesh.

Then the two doctors dexterously examined the congenital nodule on the back of Chad's head that corresponded to the biopsied tumor on James's head. They were impressed to find that it was still there, only slightly diminished in size. Jim invited me to feel it, but I opted not to. It really wasn't necessary, and I could tell Chad was reaching his limit of poking and probing. As it was, he was being very tolerant of these three strangers in his house taking such a serious interest in him.

It was approaching dinnertime, the kids were hungry, and we had gotten all of the information we could from Kathy. Time to leave. As the doctors thanked Billy and said good-bye to Chad, Kathy beckoned me into the kitchen. She carefully spread out photographs of James on the table. In the first photo I saw an adorable, curly-haired toddler on a playground. In the last was a bald, sickly, hollow-faced child who barely resembled the first. I got an empty feeling in my stomach and a knot in my heart, as any mother would, looking at the progression of change in these pictures and understanding their sad meaning. I looked over at Chad and was struck again by the mystery Kathy lived with daily, the depth of which neither of us could communicate in words. These strong and unsettling feelings stayed with me as the doctors and I drove back to Chicago.

## A Masterful Performance

We had dinner at a brightly lit Chinese restaurant across the highway from our hotel. Dr. Stevenson had a martini; Jim and I drank wine. It felt good to loosen up after a full day of travel. I was beat. But Dr. Stevenson, almost double my age, seemed as alert and awake as he was in the morning.

We talked about his research. I asked questions and Dr. Stevenson answered graciously. He paused before each answer, thinking deeply before he spoke. If he didn't have an answer to a question like, for example, "Why are there no same-family cases in Sri Lanka?" he simply said, "I don't know."

The high point of the evening for me came unexpectedly. Dr. Stevenson was talking about the latest ab-

surdity of political correctness, and I told him with
deadpan seriousness that I had heard Garrison Keillor
on the radio refer to Hillary Clinton as an "Estrogen-
American." That got him! For just a few moments he
completely lost his staid demeanor, wrinkled up his
nose, and laughed delightedly. That alone was worth
the trip!

The next day we visited Evie Redmon, an African-
American mother whose nineteen-year-old son,
Ramel, had been killed in a gang shooting in 1991. She
believed he was now back as her five-year-old son, Isaiah. She told me Isaiah had birthmarks on his chest and
arm that matched the multiple bullet wounds that
killed her first son, and that Isaiah had made some accurate statements about the murder—facts she was
sure he had no way of knowing.

I had interviewed Evie over the phone a couple of
times. It was plain that she and her two older children
believed Isaiah's was a true case of reincarnation. They
based their belief on the pattern of evidence I had seen
in other cases: some statements, some behaviors, and a
host of strange coincidences that, when all taken together, seemed convincing. And, there were the birthmarks.

The statements alone were not strong proof, since
the murder had been publicized, gone to trial, and most
likely was discussed in front of Isaiah, who was born
only three years after his brother died. When I first
brought the case to Dr. Stevenson's attention, I made it
clear that the statements were sketchy. But after he
talked to Evie, Jim thought that the chance of finding
verifiable birthmarks in an American case made it
worth their while to spend an extra day in Chicago investigating it.

Evie lived in a row of uniform, red-brick town houses situated under the approach to O'Hare Airport. She greeted us drowsily, having just gotten home from her night job a few hours earlier. Five-year-old Isaiah bounced in with a big smile, curious to see who these strange visitors were. Evie's two older children, Tania and Jacob, both tall and stylish teenagers, joined us in the living room. Evie sat in a swivel chair next to her computer desk, sipping her coffee. We three visitors settled into the long, comfortable couch facing her.

Dr. Stevenson began slowly, asking Evie to tell her story. I watched her as she gradually woke up and became more and more talkative, excited, and scattered as she jumped around in her account of Ramel's death and Isaiah's odd behaviors. Every few minutes another big jet roared just over the roof and rattled the house on its way into O'Hare, but no one seemed to notice except me. Evie's family was obviously used to it, and I could see that Dr. Stevenson couldn't be distracted once he got into the interview. I assumed that years of interviewing in third-world countries with curious villagers crowding around and animals peeking in the doorways had conditioned him to filter out distractions.

Dr. Stevenson questioned and re-questioned Evie, struggling to establish a chronology to her son's statements. He tried to determine exactly what was said when and whether Isaiah could have learned the details of his older brother's murder from overhearing family conversation. Tania and Jacob wandered in and out of the room as we spoke, stopping long enough to offer their help in corroborating Isaiah's statements and behaviors.

At first, Dr. Stevenson's challenging method made

me uncomfortable. But as he pursued his line of questioning, I realized I was witnessing a masterful performance. Without a hint of accusation or judgment, but with the right measure of steady persistence, he steered Evie repeatedly through the high points of the story, testing for and finding inconsistencies. It gradually became clear to me that Isaiah's statements could have been things he overheard his family saying, and he could have gotten cues from the family's leading questions. The statements that were so convincing to the family were beginning to look questionable under Dr. Stevenson's scrutiny.

While we were talking, Isaiah colored on the floor and hummed to himself. Tania scurried about gathering newspaper clippings of the murder, the trial, and the sentencing of the murderers. Such sad relics. I stared at Ramel's photo in the newspaper clipping of the murder. It was a high school yearbook photo of a smiling, handsome boy, full of promise.

The conversation turned, and Dr. Stevenson landed on the question of the bullet wounds. Had Evie seen the body? Did she have the autopsy report? What exactly did she know of the wounds? Then the moment of truth. With permission, Dr. Stevenson lifted Isaiah's shirt and asked Evie which marks corresponded to the bullet wounds. She pointed. Dr. Stevenson spoke softly to Jim. He called me over to look. I saw three tiny moles and one spot of light pigmentation. I scrutinized Dr. Stevenson's face for a verdict, but he was silent and poker-faced.

Evie admitted during the interview that she'd had a strong belief in reincarnation before her son's murder. Dr. Stevenson pressed her to expand on her beliefs. Did she believe it was possible for her son to return?

Yes, she did. In turn, Evie asked Dr. Stevenson if he knew anything about reincarnation. "No," he declined. I'm sure I had a surprised look on my face, and I saw the slightest smile appear on Jim's lips. I quickly deduced that Dr. Stevenson was trying to avoid an overly long visit.

As we were putting on our coats, Isaiah gallantly presented me with an apple and a miniature Christmas tree he had pulled from the closet. I was touched by his pure kindness, and explained to him that I couldn't take the Christmas tree on the plane with me. But I put the apple in my bag.

## Private Truth

We thanked Evie and her children for allowing us to visit and headed out into the blinding glare of the sun reflecting off the snow. We walked to the parking area in silence. I knew that, for Dr. Stevenson's purposes, the case had fallen apart. When we got into the car, Dr. Stevenson explained that the birthmarks were nothing but common moles, that he couldn't be sure Isaiah's statements weren't influenced by his family, and that Evie's convictions about reincarnation and her desire to have her son back may have bent her perceptions. Although some of the facts were intriguing and not easily explained, there wasn't enough objective evidence in this case to satisfy Dr. Stevenson's rigorous criteria or justify further investigation.

We headed back to our hotel. I sat quietly in the backseat, disappointed that the Redmon case hadn't panned out. While Dr. Stevenson and Jim talked about administrative issues that didn't concern me, I reflected on what had just happened. Did Dr. Stevenson's rejection of the case mean that Evie and her family were somehow mistaken and they were just wishing this so? No, it did not. Evie and her family based their belief on personal evidence that couldn't be fairly evaluated by Dr. Stevenson's methods. Still, the full story that came out of Evie's high-energy ramblings was pretty amazing. It included coincidental dates that connected her son's death and Isaiah's birth, vivid dreams, and the many small ways Isaiah mirrored Ramel's idiosyncrasies. Despite what outsiders might think, to the family these clues were convincing and real, including the simple fact that the family *felt* Ramel's presence in this new child. Did I believe this was a case of reincarnation? Based on what I had seen, there was no way for me to know for sure.

I replayed in my mind moments from the interview. As I did, it occurred to me what a valuable lesson it was to see how deftly Dr. Stevenson had handled a "weak" case. Yet I was sad that this would be my last opportunity to watch him in action. I would never get to see him interview a Suleyman or Chanai or follow him as he tracked down a child's former family to verify the child's statements. As we pulled into the hotel parking lot, I wished out loud to see an American case comparable to the best Asian cases, one with enough accurate statements and proper names that it has a chance to be solved. In more than ten years of collecting cases, I haven't found one outside the same family in which the deceased could be identified. Dr. Stevenson responded to my wish by repeating what I already knew: American children rarely give proper names, so it is almost impossible to verify who the children were in the past unless they were of the same family. In all of his years of collecting cases, he has found only a precious few "solved" American cases outside the same family. We agreed that nobody knew why. It remains an open question.[1]

## The Internet Changes Things

The next morning I was dull from lack of sleep. I had been overstimulated by all that happened the day before, and thinking about it had kept me buzzing all night. I slipped down to the hotel restaurant early and sipped earnestly at my coffee, hoping for a quick revival before the doctors appeared for breakfast. I didn't want to waste the day in a fog of fatigue. Jim walked in, looking well rested and fresh as a daisy. Within a few minutes Dr. Stevenson joined us, wide awake, suited and pressed as usual. We analyzed our options for breakfast and decided on the predictable hotel buffet.

After we settled in with our eggs and I started on my second cup of coffee, Dr. Stevenson surprised me by asking me about my work. He wanted to know what American parents wanted. What prompts a parent to contact me?

I tried to collect my thoughts and hoped that the caffeine would kick in and do its magic. I started slowly, thinking back to all the conversations I've had with mothers and fathers. I explained that, invariably, the first thing parents want is assurance that nothing is wrong with their child. They're relieved to learn their son or daughter is not an isolated nutcase—that they are not the only family with a child saying these kinds of things. Also, most American parents have never heard of children remembering past lives, and to have a relative reborn in the family sounds too crazy even to talk about. So when their child begins saying things like "remember when I was your mommy . . ." they find themselves thrust suddenly into unknown territory not covered in any parenting book. They crave guidance. They want a map to help them navigate their way through the experience and make sense of what they're seeing in their child.

Dr. Stevenson clarified, "They want advice?"

Yes, I answered. They want to know what they should do, as good parents, to respond to the past life memories. Is it better, they ask, to acknowledge what their child is saying or ignore it? Will the experience damage their child in any way? They need information, and they need counsel. Ideally, they want someone who can walk them through the process while it is happening and not after the fact. And now, I added, thanks to the Internet and the immediacy and privacy of e-mail, it's easier than ever before to give this guidance while the memories are current. A child may say something startling in the morning, and by evening the parents and I are corresponding via e-mail.

The mention of e-mail got Jim's attention. He asked me how many cases came to me through the Internet. I told him that, on average, I get two new cases a day in my e-mail or posted on the Forum, and two a week that show enough promise to warrant a follow-up telephone call. Jim's eyebrows shot up—for him, the sign of amazement. Dr. Stevenson sat eating his grapefruit, listening intently.

Emboldened by the doctors' display of enthusiasm, I forged ahead. I ventured how I thought the Internet would accelerate past life research, particularly in the West, by making it much easier to reach out to parents.

My Web site, for example, offers for the first time a single and easily accessible "place" where families can report their reincarnation experiences and get help.[2] Before e-mail and the Internet, if a family had a child with obvious past life memories, who could they talk to? As one mother said to me recently, "If I go to the priest, he'll try to exorcise it; if I go to the psychiatrist, he'll try to fix it."

But now, anyone who has access to a computer can type a few words into a search engine and get the information and encouragement they need. I've put enough basic information on my Web site to get people started. And because the Internet is interactive, the communication goes both ways. For example, in the Reincarnation Forum on my Web site, families exchange information, ask questions, and discover together how similar their experiences are.

I predicted that due to the Internet, the trickle of Western cases we're seeing now will grow exponentially. This could revolutionize the study of reincarnation as we collect enough Western cases to understand what is peculiar to the phenomenon in our Judeo-Christian culture. And maybe, with a much bigger sample of cases to work with, we will finally begin to see American cases with the kind of detailed memories and proper names we find only in Asian cases now.

The doctors nodded thoughtfully. I could see they were both taking in everything I was saying and turning it over in their minds.

## Love Is Enough

Soon it was time to leave Chicago. Jim and Dr. Stevenson dropped me off at the USAir terminal, and we said our good-byes. I collapsed in my seat, body tired, caffeinated mind awake. As the plane waited on the ground, biding its time before takeoff, I closed my eyes and reflected on all that had happened in the last forty-eight hours.

This trip had given me valuable perspective on the direction of my work. I've known for a long time that verifying past life memories is not my primary aim— Dr. Stevenson and his colleagues have already done a superb job of that. But now I'm more convinced than ever that my mission is to go to the next stage and work with the subjective issues and practical implications that Dr. Stevenson does not address.

Building on Dr. Stevenson's foundation, I'm free to work with the many cases that aren't as strong in objective evidence, but still have much to teach. Same-family cases, for example. And most American cases, for that matter. There are so many practical lessons, so much insight, still to be gathered from these cases. There is so much to be discovered about the implications of children's past life memories in the context of modern American culture. I can see how someday, as the number of cases grows and reincarnation gains respectability, the past life perspective could turn psychology and child development upside down. At the very least, the stories cast the parent-child relationship in a whole new light. All the things that the parents in these cases are figuring out on their own need to be understood, articulated, and organized into practical advice all parents can use. Judging by my e-mail, the need is there and growing every day.

And there is a higher mystical and spiritual level to these reincarnation cases that Dr. Stevenson doesn't pursue in his writings. I know the stories have the power to change people. In case after case, parents tell me how their child's experience dissolved their own fear of death. But the spiritual benefit is not for parents alone. The stories are full of clues for *anyone* who has ever wondered what happens after death, or who has ever felt an instant soul connection when meeting a person for the first time. These higher lessons need to be shared as well.

My mind was so lost in thought, it hadn't really registered that the plane had taken off. The sun's glare suddenly pierced the tiny window and hit my face as the plane broke through the clouds. Staring out the window at the rolling floor of clouds below me, I sank back into my thoughts. I recalled a revealing moment in the car just before we parted at O'Hare. Jim was driving, Dr. Stevenson navigating, and I was in the backseat fretting that time was running out for me to ask questions. I didn't know when I would see Dr. Stevenson again, and I had one more question I was wrestling with. I leaned forward between the two front seats to be heard above the car noise. I told Dr. Stevenson I had been working on a chapter called "Choosing a Life," and I wanted to know what his latest thoughts were on the question of why we pick the parents we do. I prefaced my question by rattling off his published observations on the topic, proving that I had done my homework and wasn't being lazy. I ticked off the reasons: geography, familiarity, randomness, unfinished business, and the idea that love may draw a soul to its parents.

I heard him mumble, with the slightest edge in his voice, "Isn't love reason *enough*?"

Not the answer I was expecting from this man of science.

# Chapter 5

## Mother Switching

*I feel sad for my mother. She had a miserable child-hood, and because of her addictions she never had a good relationship with any of us. What a wasted life! Now I feel that if Katie is my mom, she gets another kick at the cat, another chance to try to figure it out. I think that's why she's back.*

A close relationship between two people does not have to end forever when one of them dies. If they are reunited by reincarnation, the relationship resumes. Of course, the relationship can never be exactly the same as it was before. But something of the *quality* of the former relationship does carry over, as it does when any two people come together after a long absence: Some things change, some things don't change.

Mother-switching—cases in which a mother dies and is reborn to her own daughter—is a dramatic illustration of how relationships can continue despite death.

The mother-child bond, forged in the act of birth, is the most primary, the most emotionally charged, and sometimes the most difficult relationship for any of us. So when a mother dies and returns to her daughter, it can be a celebration of renewed love, a reunion that deepens the soulful bond nurtured throughout the previous life. Or it can revive the phantom pains of old emotional injuries and grudges that remained unhealed when Mother died. (I have not included father-switching cases in this chapter, but they do exist, and the same principles apply.)

If your own mother returned as your child, how would you feel? Your answer, I'm sure, would reflect the tone of your relationship with her. Would you be grateful without reservation to have her back? Or would you be uneasy, afraid you would push each other's buttons as you did before?

The four mother-switching stories in this chapter give you an opportunity to follow each mother through her unique process of discovery. The first two stories are of loving relationships that carried forward after death; the last two bring up the darker side of relationships, when two abusive mothers return in need of forgiveness from the very people they hurt before. These stories have moments that are funny and endearing, as when for instance a pint-size two-year-old pulls rank and tries to boss around her mother as she did in the past. Other times, the remarks and behaviors of the child are disturbing and unsettling, as they resurrect nasty conflicts from the past.

Through these mother-switching stories you will see how recognizing the truth of your child's reincarnation can have benefits for both you and your child. The role reversal provides a unique perspective on the soul identity of your child, your former mother. Since you are intimately acquainted with your mother's personality—her strengths and weaknesses—you are in a position to recognize these qualities if they reappear in your daughter or son. With this special awareness, you can step back and understand which behaviors and attitudes your child brought with her from the past. This perspective allows you to be more patient and compassionate when confronted with old and familiar conflicts, and it gives you insight as how best to guide your child into new patterns of behavior. It is an opportunity for the child to learn and grow beyond what she was before.

For you, now the mother, the benefit can be greater self-understanding. Your child might trigger emotional issues stemming from your relationship with your deceased mother. Now, parenting your own mother gives you a blessed second chance to face some of these issues and help you move ahead in your own life.

## *"Chattanooga Choo Choo" (Candy Mott)*

I choose to start off with Candy Mott's mother-switching story because it's so full of delight. It's a story of a singing, dancing, super-mom who dies and returns, with personality and talents almost completely intact, as her own singing, dancing, nonstop granddaughter. Candy, the mother in the middle, admired her mother and is happy to have her back. The switch in roles also gives her a chance to learn patience and accommodation, and it grants her mother's dying wish to know her daughter better.

Candy adored her mother, Artise. Artise worked as

an accountant, but also had a flamboyant and theatrical side to her. She sang all the time, any chance she could get, and she loved to dance. She taught dance in their California community and performed regularly in the local theater. She was one of those multitalented people who have a gift for doing ten things at once, and doing them all well. She was a devoted mother to Candy and her younger brother, who had been sickly since birth.

When Candy was thirteen, her father died suddenly. From then on, Artise was the sole support of the family, and had to divide her attention between her career and her two children.

About twenty years after her husband died, Artise was diagnosed with breast cancer and had to move in with Candy. Candy did her best to care for her dying mother, but didn't feel up to the task because she was already stretched to the limit raising two kids, including a demanding two-year-old. The added responsibilities of caring for a sick mother overwhelmed her. One day she was so frustrated and frazzled she told Artise that she couldn't keep up the pace any longer. Artise, in an attempt to bolster Candy's spirit, reminded her that "God only makes you deal with what you can handle."

Candy pleaded, "Then don't die today, because I can't handle it today."

Her mother, who was a believer in reincarnation, responded cryptically, "After I die, I'm going to be back. I'll be back to see you again."

Candy didn't quite understand what her mother meant. Would she come back as a ghost or in her dreams? She didn't know. But since Artise was so close to death and so weak, Candy humored her and said, "I can hardly wait!"

Two weeks later Artise died. By then, they were both ready.

In the fall of 1985, Candy was going through a particularly rough time. Her marriage was falling apart and she was sick for a month with flulike symptoms. When her doctor informed her that she wasn't sick but pregnant, she couldn't believe it. She had had a miscarriage after her second child was born and was told at the time that she couldn't have any more children because her tubes were blocked. Although the doctors warned her that having another baby could be dangerous to her and the child, Candy decided to go ahead with the "miracle" pregnancy. She believed God wanted her to have this child and it would be all right. Five months later Candy gave birth to a perfectly healthy, five-pound baby girl she named Kari.

Candy will never forget that moment:

> When they brought Kari to me for the first time, my husband and my grandmother (Artise's mother, Dolores) were with me too. We all saw it right away. Kari looked just like Artise! Her eyes, especially, had that twinkle that Artise was famous for. My husband said it was heredity, but Dolores and I suspected it was more than that. I wondered at the time if my mother's prediction had come to pass.
>
> Even before Kari could talk, everyone in the family saw the similarities between her and Artise. From the time she was nine months old, before she could walk, Kari would sit in her playpen and hum old tunes I couldn't identify. But Dolores would say, "Oh, that's so-and-so," and go to the piano and play the melody, to Kari's utter delight. Kari would actually *hum along* and swing her arms to the music. She would just

beam! This absolutely floored my grandmother, because she recognized them as tunes my mother had sung. Artise sang all of the time and performed every chance she got—at weddings, in musicals, in the supermarket—anywhere. We could count on her to embarrass us by singing and dancing in the aisles at church!

Kari was precocious in other ways too. She talked in full sentences by thirteen months. She startled me and her grandparents by saying and doing things that exactly mimicked Artise's distinctive personality. At these moments when Artise shone through Kari, we would all roll our eyes and laugh. "Oh, my God! She's doing it again."

At first, seeing Kari as a miniature Artise was nothing more than a family entertainment and her antics were accepted as typical one-year-old cuteness. Although they joked that Kari was the reincarnation of Artise, no one took the idea too seriously. Until, that is, a series of incidents when Kari was just two years old thoroughly convinced them Kari was the reincarnation of Artise. From that time on, it was no longer a joke, but something real they lived with and enjoyed every day. Candy remembers what happened:

One day Dolores and I went shopping; and, of course, we took two-year-old Kari with us. We were driving down the road with her in the back in her car seat humming merrily as usual. Suddenly she burst into song, singing the old standard "Chattanooga Choo Choo" word for word! I was so unnerved I couldn't drive. I pulled over so I wouldn't wreck the car. We all just sat there on the side of the road until Kari finished *all* the verses. My poor grandmother was almost in hysterics, muttering, "Oh, my God! Oh, my God!"

I asked Dolores, "Didn't Grandfather always sing that song?" I remembered him singing it to us when we rode in his car.

"Yes," she said, "it was one of his and Artise's favorite songs." There was no way Kari could have known the verses. She had never heard the song before, not from the radio or TV—it's not a song you hear anymore. And she didn't get it from me. I was vaguely aware of the song, but I sure didn't know all of the verses and neither did Dolores. But this little two-year-old knew all of them, every line!

A short time after this, I was shopping in the supermarket with Kari, who was sitting in the grocery cart. It was almost nap time and she was getting cranky and acting up. I lost my patience and scolded, "Kari, please sit still, don't grab the yogurt, and don't throw things out of the cart!"

Kari gave me a piercing look and talked back in her squeaky voice, "When you were little, you used to do the same thing and you never got in trouble!"

A tall, slender woman I didn't know overheard our tiff, approached us, and said very matter-of-factly, "You know who your little girl is, don't you? She's your mother!"

I lost it, and snapped, "I know she's my mother and she's driving me crazy!"

I was so distracted by Kari's behavior, the tall woman's remark didn't register until she had disappeared down the aisle, leaving me speechless by the dairy case. I found out later, when telling a friend the story of this bizarre encounter, that the tall woman was a well-known psychic who did past life readings.

As Kari grew and her personality developed, Candy and her grandmothers noticed how much the child's temperament was like Artise's.

Kari is so different from my other two children. She is boisterous, outspoken, and has a fierce temper, just like my mother used to have. In her behavior and attitude too, she resembles Artise. When it comes to clothes and appearance, I'm strictly a jeans-and-T-shirt type of person. Kari, on the other hand, is compulsive about fashion and always fussing about wearing what she thinks are just the right clothes, accessories, and makeup. She plays dress-up all the time and wears costumes that are outrageous and theatrical. Artise loved dressing up and all the trappings of stage performance—especially the costumes and makeup.

When I took four-year-old Kari to her first tap-dance class, she flitted across the floor as if she knew exactly what she was doing. The teacher was astounded as she watched her run through complicated steps and postures. She asked me, "Has that child already had lessons?"

I knew I couldn't tell her the whole truth, so I told her, "Oh, yes, she's done it before."—while chuckling to myself: "Of course she knows how to do this. My mother was a dance teacher."

Kari recognized objects that had belonged to my mother. Once, when she was playing dress-up, she went into my makeup and put bright red lipstick all over her face, smacked her lips, and said to Dolores, who was sewing nearby, "What do you think?"

Amused, Dolores said, "Kari, that's lovely, and where did you get the lipstick?"

Kari replied, "This is mine," and held out a white

porcelain tube. Dolores looked carefully at Candy's big collection of lipsticks. There were about fifty different lipsticks she could have picked up, including some with more attractive tubes. But Kari knew this particular one was one of the few that had belonged to Artise.

When Kari was five, Dolores died. After her death, Kari and I sorted through her accumulated possessions of eighty-six years. As we picked through knick-knacks, crystal, and household items, Kari surprised me with her comments about the origins and uses of certain things. I would point to a vase and ask, "I wonder where Grandma got that?"

Without hesitating, Kari would say, "It was a Christmas gift." And she would be right. I would remember that it had been something Artise gave to Dolores for Christmas.

If I couldn't identify something in the collection, I would ask Kari, "I wonder what that is?" and Kari would have an answer. Once, she looked at a gadget I couldn't identify and announced, "That's a knife sharpener."

It didn't look like a knife sharpener to me, so I asked her, "How do you know?"

In an exasperated voice she replied, "Well, get me a knife and I'll show you!"

When Kari picked out certain items she said she wanted—crystal and select pieces of jewelry—I put them in boxes to save for her when she got older. Every one of them was something that had a connection to Artise and still held meaning for Kari. I felt I had to honor that.

When I first interviewed Candy, Kari was already a young teenager. I was impressed with Candy's lighthearted attitude and her matter-of-fact acceptance of her daughter as the reincarnation of her mother. It all seemed quite normal to her. I was curious, though, how Kari felt about this now that she was a teen. Candy explained, "Kari is aware of who she is. Sometimes she'll ask me, 'Am I really like Grandma?' I will answer yes, but not make a big deal about it. But when she does something or says something just like my mother, I will get a look on my face and roll my eyes, and Kari knows that she's floored me."

Knowing who Kari is has helped Candy be a better and more understanding mother—especially as Kari enters her teens.

Kari seems to get upset more easily these days, beyond the normal difficulties of being a teen. I can see she sometimes feels frustrated, caught between two different realities—caught between what she knows from her past life and what she has to do in this life. She thinks it's stupid to do certain things because she's already done them and there's no point in doing them again.

For example, she won't study for tests, but she aces them anyway. She likes to read cookbooks, she adores cooking, and she likes to do other "old lady" things. It helps me understand her behavior if I think of her as a child from my mom's time trying to cope with the pressures of being a teenager in the 1990s. She doesn't understand why things are so complicated and why kids are so mean today.

Candy's mother, you will recall, had been a believer in reincarnation, and just before her death she had alluded to returning. I asked Candy why she thought her mother wanted to return to the family so quickly after death.

Just before my mother died, she told me, "I'm honestly very sorry I didn't get to know you. I've always been proud of you, and I think you're wonderful and you do fine things, but I feel like I've been shortchanged." She told me this four days before she died!

I told her, "This is a fine time to tell me I'm an okay person. Why did you wait all of these years to tell me this?" I was very angry with her for waiting until the last minute to give me her approval and attention. So I really believe she came back partly to make it up to me and to get to know me better. Now we have plenty of time to continue our relationship.

In so many ways, Kari has brought my mother's fierce personality with her into this life. I think that's partly for my benefit, because her stubbornness and assertiveness are forcing me to learn patience and tolerance. When I was younger, before I had Kari, I always had to do things my way. I was very strong-willed with my mother, and she often had to give in just to make things easier. I now see myself in the same situation with Kari, but this time the roles are reversed. I have to slow down and look at things differently—to look at the other side—which is very hard for me. This is what she's teaching me. I have to learn to compromise and give a little. Looking at this situation from another angle gives me a chance to make the relationship more balanced.

It's funny, though, sometimes I get frustrated because I feel I'm trying to reason with Kari and my mother at the same time. I have to remind myself she's the child this time. This can be refreshing, too. Because she has such a strong sense of self and is so self-directed and determined, she commands respect. I always tell her how proud I am of these qualities, and I always support her ability to make good choices. These are the things my mother never had a chance to tell me until right before she died. I now know how important it is for me to acknowledge her while she is still young.

I believe that people come back to learn lessons. So it's a major responsibility to know my mother is back as my daughter, that she has come back to learn certain things, and that I have a role in helping her. It's special to know that together we're evolving and growing as souls even through different lives. I feel very lucky to know this really can happen.

## Signals of Love (Cece Klepper)

Technically, this is a case of a grandmother, not a mother, coming back as a daughter. But because, for reasons explained in the case, Cece was closer to her grandmother than she was to her mother, it works as a mother-switching case.

This is another case where a little girl was constantly saying and doing funny, surprising things that reminded the family who she had been in the past. In addition, it is notable for the recognitions of people and places from the past life the little girl made, another sign of a past life memory.

Cece and her grandmother, Oscelia, became best friends when she was seven, when Cece's younger sister was born, and her mother's attention shifted to the new baby. A few years later, Cece's parents' marriage was deteriorating, and they became increasingly wound up in their own serious adult problems. Oscelia became Cece's substitute parent, and Cece spent her afternoons with her. Oscelia showered the child with love and attention.

But when Cece was in her early teens, Oscelia moved to sunny Florida to get away from the Massachusetts winters. Cece missed her terribly. Oscelia did return to Massachusetts for a while when Cece was a teenager to care for her while her parents were battling through a divorce. Oscelia was Cece's only friend and anchor during this turbulent time. Shortly after Oscelia returned to Florida, she became ill. She died in October 1966, when Cece was sixteen.

Cece mourned her grandmother as if her own mother had died. She was angry at her for dying because she felt Oscelia had abandoned her when she needed her comfort and support the most. Cece began having disturbing dreams in which her grandmother was always going away, always leaving her alone. With time, the dreams stopped and Cece's anger subsided. But the profound longing to be with her grandmother again never went away.

The dreams of her grandmother resumed when Cece became pregnant in 1973. But in these dreams, Oscelia was always coming toward her, not going away. Cece would wake up from these vivid dreams feeling her grandmother's familiar, loving presence wrapped around her. Then, during the seventh month of pregnancy, the dreams stopped. At about the same time, Cece began to sense her grandmother's presence in a different way. She would often get a sudden whiff of Oscelia's distinctive sweet odor—a combination of Dove soap and Noxzema—around the house. She tried, but couldn't isolate any source or find a rational explanation for these smells. They were there one minute, strong and unmistakable, and gone the next.

Cece began to wonder if her grandmother might be returning as the child she was carrying. This prospect made her very happy, but it confused her too. In the books on reincarnation she had read, Cece got the idea that a soul was required to wait a long time in heaven before returning, and her grandmother had been gone only seven years. Nothing she had ever read said it was possible to return to the same family. The only options for rebirth, as far as she could gather, were remote and impersonal.

But Cece forgot all about what the books said when she held her newborn daughter, Dee, for the first time. She was overwhelmed with feelings of familiarity.

> The feeling was so incredible. In a rush I had that wonderful feeling again that I used to have when I was with Oscelia. I looked at Dee's face and thought, "I wish I knew if you really were my grandmother, Oscelia." Suddenly this little one opened her eyes, looked directly into mine, and made a face just like my grandmother used to make when she was clowning around. From that moment on, I never again longed for my grandmother. Yet, at the same time, I didn't think of Dee as anyone but my own baby.

Cece became so completely absorbed in being a mother and caring for Dee that she didn't think about Oscelia or the overwhelming feeling of familiarity she had experienced at Dee's birth. Believing that her baby was her grandmother reborn was just too far-fetched to dwell on for long. Just before Dee turned two, however, she started saying and doing things that made Cece wonder.

I vividly remember the day. Dee was about twenty months old and I was pregnant with my son. We were shopping for groceries and Dee was sitting in the shopping cart. I had my back turned as I reached to take something off the shelf. I heard Dee squeal with pleasure as a woman talked to her in a kind voice. "Aren't you the cutest little girl." I turned and saw a look of sheer delight on my daughter's face, and she was waving her arms and feet in the air. If she hadn't been strapped in her seat, she would have jumped into that lady's arms.

Dee squealed again. "Look, Mommy, my old friend is here!" The way she said it sent a chill through me and made me look carefully for the first time at this tiny, elderly lady who was at eye level with my daughter in the shopping cart.

Suddenly I thought I recognized her too. "Mrs. Berger?" I ventured.

She replied in a familiar Yiddish accent, "Yes, it's me."

I couldn't believe it! Mrs. Berger had been my grandmother's neighbor for thirty-five years before she moved to Florida. I hadn't seen her since I was about six years old.

It was after this incident that I began to believe, for the first time since those distinctive odors filled my house during my pregnancy, that Dee might actually be my grandmother. I allowed myself to think, "Wow, maybe I'm not just imagining all this!"

Even though Cece began to believe that Dee was her grandmother reborn, she was careful not to jump to conclusions. She was aware that her longing to be reunited with Oscelia might cause her to impose her grandmother's identity on her daughter. So she tried to observe objectively what Dee offered spontaneously and not overreact or ask leading questions. She didn't want to create something that wasn't there or put ideas in the child's head. She wanted to let the truth come out on its own.

Over the next few months Dee's recognitions and past life memories became more frequent. At the same time, paradoxically, it became less important for Cece to know for sure if Dee was her grandmother. "It's hard to explain, but I felt that these telltale behaviors and remarks were meant to be signals, not proof. Through them, Dee was affirming to me my grandmother's undying love. I simply loved Dee for who she was. And that was enough."

But then a few months after Dee's second birthday, she did something that clinched it for Cece.

We went shopping in a department store in Springfield. I decided to treat Dee to a new experience—a visit to the store's tearoom on the mezzanine. It was one of my favorite places to visit with Oscelia when I was a little girl. As soon as we walked off the elevator, Dee chirped, "I like this place!" We sat down at a lunch table and an elderly waitress approached. Dee called out brightly, "Here comes Helen!" When the waitress got close enough for me to read her name tag, I saw that Dee was correct.

I asked Dee, "How did you know her name?"

"I used to come here when I was big, and I remember Helen from before," she said, beaming at her old "friend."

Dee's remark made the waitress very uncomfortable—how could this cute little girl recognize her if she had never seen her before? I was a little surprised myself, but by this time I was used to the idea that Dee was my grandmother and this was just the final confirmation.

## Appropriate Roles

In cases of same-family reincarnation, recognitions of strangers outside a child's family, such as Mrs. Berger and the waitress Helen, provide some of the best evidence that the child is truly remembering a past life. This is because so much in the family environment looks the same to the child, and there is little to trigger a sudden recognition. But when a two- or three-year-old encounters for the first time someone *outside* her immediate surroundings whom she recognizes from her past life, she responds appropriately, as Dee did in the supermarket and the tearoom. To the child, it's simply a reunion after a long absence. To the child's parent or grandparent, it's a total shock.

In many of Dr. Stevenson's best cases, children spontaneously recognize total strangers as former family members or acquaintances. When they do, there is always a congruence between how the child reacts and the quality of the previous relationship. Upon seeing a beloved former spouse or parent, the child might be so happy he is moved to tears or jumps into the lap of this seeming "stranger" and hugs and kisses him or her. Or when some of these three- or four-year-old children chance on their murderers from a previous life in a crowded market, they tremble with fear or vow revenge and throw stones at them. Clearly, all is not forgotten or forgiven after death. The tenor of the relationship tends to remain the same.

In mother-switching cases, children often identify so strongly with their former roles that they continue to pull rank. Cece vividly remembers instances of this with Dee.

Between Dee's second and third birthdays, her memories were very active and she did something new almost every day that reminded me of Oscelia. Sometimes when I reprimanded her for mischief she had done, the little imp in diapers would get this patient and long-suffering look on her face and respond, "You really shouldn't talk to me like that because I used to take care of you when I was big." She was clearly implying she still had authority over me and that I should just "buzz off!" I had to control my laughter at the absurdity of this! It got to the point where I would just chuckle and say to myself, "Oh, well, there's another sign she knows who she is."

A sense of humor is well advised in these cases!

In the same way that children remember people from a past life, they can remember places. This phenomenon is common enough that it has a name: *landmark memories*. If a child sees for the first time a place familiar to him or her from the past, it can trigger images and resonant feelings and cause a sudden reaction. The parent is totally surprised by the strong emotions that seem to come out of nowhere. But when this happens, the clues that link the site to the past life are usually not hard to discover.

Dee recognized the mezzanine tearoom in the department store and was delighted. A little later she had another landmark memory that was not pleasant, but traumatic.

When Dee was two and memories and signs were popping up almost daily, I was driving her to a play group at a new friend's house, traveling down streets she had never been on before. We paused at a stop sign and she suddenly burst into tears and sobbed hysterically. Her outburst scared me, and I asked, "What's wrong, sweetie?"

She answered through her tears, "Oh, you have to be very careful here. It's very dangerous here. This is where you get hurt." She calmed down as soon as the intersection was out of sight.

I thought this very strange and mentioned it to my mother, identifying the intersection by its cross streets. My mother knew immediately why that intersection was significant: Oscelia had been in a serious car accident at that corner in 1960, when I was nine. One of my cousins was with her in the front seat, and when Oscelia saw they were about to collide with another car, she threw herself over the child and took the full impact of the crash. My cousin was okay, but Oscelia's arm was seriously injured and didn't heal for a long time.

Apparently Dee had a little catharsis that day when she cried at the intersection, because the next time we went through it, she was fine. She never mentioned it again.

As Dee grew older, her direct statements and recognitions from the past faded. But pieces of her memories as Oscelia continued to poke through from time to time. Cece recalled an incident when Dee was about four, the full significance of which didn't emerge until years later.

One day a friend gave us three kittens because she knew Dee loved animals. Dee insisted on naming them Jenny, Leila, and Lester. I asked her why she chose those names, pointing to Lester, a red tabby. She replied, "Because he looks like a Lester." I didn't think too much of it at the time except to wonder if the fact that Oscelia's sister's name was Jenny had anything to do with the cat's name. Then, just last year, my mother sent us our family genealogy that she's been compiling. In going through the charts, I noticed Oscelia's sister's name was really Jenny Leila and she had a brother named Lester, whom I didn't know at all. When I read that I got these little prickles all over my body. Soon after, when I pointed out the "coincidence" of the cats' names to a visiting relative, he added, "Lester had bright red hair."

Now that Dee is an adult, how does Cece feel about parenting her own grandmother?

I'm delighted we are back together again in the same family. We have a deep underlying love that got us through some difficult times. Overall, our relationship has been very positive; we've helped each other a lot.

I asked Cece *why* she thought her grandmother had come back to her. She immediately gave me the reason I hear most often: longing for love.

I feel that she came back to me because I missed her terribly and really needed her. I really think my longing to be with her again drew her back to me.

But it wasn't one-sided. She came back to learn too. Oscelia used to carry grudges for a very long time; she rarely forgave people. And Dee's the same way. I'm just the opposite. I'm more able to see things from the

other person's point of view. I'm helping Dee with
that now, beginning with her father. She was the apple
of her daddy's eye until we divorced and lost everything. She was so enraged she's barely spoken to him
since. I'm urging her to change that pattern and make
peace with him. She's trying, but it isn't easy for her.

In another way, Dee has already changed. Oscelia
was very prejudiced against black people. When Dee
was in seventh grade, I dated an African-American
man from work. Dee said to me, "Oh, Peter is the
nicest man, but how can you stand being with someone who is black?" Ironically, Dee is now engaged to
a Jamaican man.

Cece had an interesting realization about role reversal when her grandmother reincarnated as her daughter.

I prefer the relationship with my daughter compared
to my relationship with my grandmother because it
feels more comfortable. I always felt older than my
grandmother and felt that I knew more than she did. I
always felt protective of her too. Our present roles are
more appropriate for the kind of feelings that are there
between us. Now it feels more natural, more fitting, to
be her mother than her granddaughter.

## The Sins of the Mothers

In the last two cases, we saw how warm, loving, and
positive feelings can transcend death and set the tone
for new and harmonious relationships. The mothers,
Candy and Cece, were delighted to be reunited with
souls they had loved and missed so much. But not all

relationships are sweet and loving. Some are down-right rancorous.

Indeed, we would all like to believe that anger, hatred, and old disputes are canceled at death. It is comforting to believe that in heaven our slates are wiped clean before we return. There is evidence from some of Dr. Stevenson's cases that errant souls can and do change, reform, and become more loving from one life to the next. But there is also evidence that bad feelings and old grudges remain intact and reemerge when the deceased is reborn as a new child. Specific issues can carry forward into the next life, causing friction and misunderstanding.

This type of negative carryover probably happens often, but if it is not recognized as a past life pattern, it can be perplexing to parents. They don't understand why their child is distant or antagonistic. And they may blame themselves, question their parenting skills, and wonder why this child acts so differently toward them than their other children do. But when these attitudes can be traced to a specific past life relationship and not to anything that the parents did wrong, it can be a step toward resolution and healing.

In the following two cases, abusive mothers are reborn to their daughters. The outcomes of these two cases prove that a soul does not necessarily have to pay for its sins in one life with punishment in the next. Apparently the universe is kinder than that. These souls returned to their own daughters to be forgiven and loved.

The first is a case of gender switching as well as mother switching: The mother reincarnates not as a girl, but as a boy. This child brings with him the same abusive tendencies he had in his previous life. When the mother, Sarah Holden, finally understands who this child had been in the past—her own mother—she is able to practice forgiveness and help this soul break a destructive pattern.

## The Two Sides of Margaret (Sarah Holden)

To people who didn't know her well, Margaret was an energetic, creative, and active woman with a flair for design. But to her family she was hateful, angry, and domineering. She told everyone what to do with their lives and was viciously critical of everything. Nothing anyone did was good enough for her. Margaret herself had been beaten when she was a child, and she perpetuated this tradition of cruelty. She abused all four of her children physically, mentally, and emotionally. Her husband couldn't stand up to her and never lifted a hand to protect the children from his wife's wrath.

Sarah, the youngest of the children, was a prisoner of her mother's abuse throughout her entire childhood. When she was two, her mother was confined to bed with emphysema, the consequence of a lifetime of chain-smoking. Sarah quickly adapted to the situation by being the "perfect" child, taking care at all times to avoid giving her mother cause to punish her. She also learned to keep her distance—well outside of her mother's striking range.

In the year before her death, Margaret softened and her relationship with Sarah began to change. Ironically, after all those years of hate and abuse, they began to form a loving relationship. They talked a lot and Margaret, for the first time, began to take a genuine interest in Sarah's life without criticizing her. Sarah was engaged to be married and Margaret adored her fiancé. She took a great interest in helping Sarah plan the wedding and design her wedding dress. But she died in 1990, missing the wedding by two months.

Despite the brief reprieve at the end, Sarah was scarred from the years of abuse. She went into therapy after her mother's death to deal with the many problems from her childhood. She knew if she didn't address her feelings, she would unconsciously continue the tradition of abuse with her own children, and she was terrified that she would become like her mother. She was determined to give her children the love and positive attention she had never known. After two years of hard work in therapy, she felt she had turned her life around and had finally accepted the difficult circumstances of her childhood and had forgiven her mother.

Within a year of her marriage, Sarah had her first son, Kyle. Her second son, Miles, was born in late 1992.

At first, Miles was an affectionate and docile baby, but as soon as he became verbal, his contentious personality began to show. He and Sarah fought constantly. They didn't just fight over certain issues—they fought over everything. This was not the usual two-year-old "me-mine-no" assertive behavior most parents deal with, either. Miles continually berated his mother, telling her everything she did was wrong. For example, when she tried to do art projects with him, he would criticize her every step of the way, taking all the fun out of it. It didn't matter what Sarah tried, Miles simply would not accept her authority and made it his mission to undermine and belittle her. There were many days when Sarah didn't even want to be around her own son because he made her feel so bad about herself.

Sarah reflects on her feelings at the time:

Being with Miles felt exactly like being with my mother. Everyone who knew my mom used to call her the "Queen Bee." She was a little dictator—she always had to be the boss and found fault with everything. And it was exactly the same with Miles. At school and anywhere else, everyone would say he's an angel. When I tried to tell them the way he acted with us, they would say, "No way!" My mom was just like that—her outward appearance was totally different from the way she acted with us. People used to say, "Oh, what a wonderful lady she is; how lucky you are to have her as your mother." And we used to think, "You have no idea what we're living with!"

Sarah blamed herself for Miles's behavior. She thought back to all the therapy she had undergone in order to understand and change her own attitudes. She believed the positive and loving relationship she had with her older son, Kyle, was the result of the emotional repair she had accomplished in therapy. So what happened with Miles? Was it some kind of unresolved, negative feelings she still had that were unconsciously influencing his behavior? She didn't know. It was a mystery.

Curiously, after each of his episodes of insult and psychological abuse, Miles would ask his mother, "If I'm bad, will you still love me? Will you *always* love me?" He asked her this all the time. Sarah couldn't tell if it was a ploy to avoid punishment or if he was really concerned that she would reject him.

## Obsessed with Elephants

There were other, more benign things about Miles that reminded Sarah of her mother. The most remarkable similarity was his passion for animals—especially for elephants. It was clear from very early on that Miles was obsessed with elephants. Anytime his mother took him shopping and he saw an elephant in any form— stuffed, printed, or molded—he would scream until she bought it for him. His room was a shrine to the beast. Sarah thought this odd, because her mother too collected elephant figurines and prints; she had elephants on every shelf and wall of her bedroom, where she spent most of her time. Everyone knew that all they had to do to please Margaret on any special occasion was to give her an elephant-related gift. But Miles never knew any of this. He had never seen her house or her collection.

Then one incident triggered Sarah's recognition of the truth, and she understood the connection between Miles and her mother.

One day when he was four, Miles and I were shopping in the mall when he spotted a poster print of an elephant. He begged and begged me to buy it for him. He repeated without letup, "I need it! I need it!"

I was in a hurry and thought I could win this one. I said, "No, you have enough elephants in your room." But he was more adamant than usual for this particular print. Finally, I gave in and bought it.

He was delighted with the print, and as soon as we got home, he ran into his bedroom and hung it on the wall over his bed.

A few days later my father, Margaret's husband,

came for a visit. Miles met him at the door and dragged him into his bedroom to show off his newest elephant picture. He was so proud of it. Immediately my father exclaimed, "My God! That's a Robert Bateman print! He was your grandmother's favorite artist!"

My jaw must have hit the floor, I was so surprised. Suddenly it all made sense.

Sarah's father made the connection first. Perhaps because he did not see Miles every day, as Sarah did, he could be objective about the similarities between Miles and his deceased wife. He saw them not as coincidence, but as reincarnation. Then Sarah saw it too, and the family began to think back and piece things together in this new light. In the context of reincarnation, Miles's atrocious behavior began to make sense, as did his obsession with elephants and his frequent question, "If I'm bad, will you still love me? Will you *always* love me?" These repeated queries now fit the pattern. For if Miles were really her mother, perhaps her mother's soul needed reassurance that she would be loved in spite of her horrible behavior in the past.

Looking at Miles as the reincarnation of Margaret, Sarah's feelings shifted completely.

For so long I've felt like such a rotten mother because of all the anger between Miles and me. I always blamed myself for our difficult relationship. But now that I accept the possibility that he is my mom, I know why he acts the way he does. Even though my mother began to change before her death, she really never got over all the hurt and pain of her own childhood, and she still harbored a lot of anger.

Now I no longer blame myself for Miles's behavior

or believe that his anger is the result of something I've done or not done. And now that I'm not blaming myself, I can be more patient in helping him work things out, rather than pushing him away, which is how I dealt with him before. I just couldn't handle the similarities between him and my mother—they were too much for me.

Putting all of this in the perspective of reincarnation, I see Miles's behavior as an opportunity to help my mother's soul finally break the cycle of abuse, which she was unable to do with her children in her lifetime. I've already done a lot of hard work in therapy because of our relationship, and I now feel ready to help her—through Miles. I think that's exactly why she came back to me as my son: so we could both heal, grow, and learn what it's like to be supportive and positive and not fight all the time.

And I think that there is a reason why she came back to me and not to one of my siblings. As much as she and I clashed, and in spite of all of our problems, we still had a strong connection. Since I was the youngest child, I got the least of her abuse, and because she was bedridden when I was only two, there were so many things she couldn't do with me. We both missed out on a lot together.

At the end of her life she trusted me more than the others, probably because she treated the others worse than she treated me and felt the least guilty in our relationship. When she died, she left her wedding rings to me because she knew I was the only one in the family who wouldn't pawn them. She adored my husband and was so pleased we were getting married. She was planning all the decorations and dresses for my wedding, but she died before she could see it. So, in her way, I think she felt guilty that she was letting me down once again.

Now Miles is six, and he and his mother have a wonderful, loving relationship. Sarah feels they've finally broken the cycle of abuse. Sarah notes with pleasure that her mother's good qualities now predominate in Miles, especially her sensitivity toward animals and her flair for design. For example, Margaret loved decorating the house. Miles's favorite TV show is one about house decorating. One day the six-year-old went into his bedroom, lifted up the carpet, and explained to his mother, "Mom, this is a wood floor. I can paint my floor." Sarah was amused because this was exactly what her mother would have done.

Miles is also very attached to his collection of stuffed dogs—he always chooses black ones and names all of them "Newf." It recently occurred to Sarah that when her mother was young, she bred show dogs—Newfoundlands, which are black.

Sarah adds, "The similarities are clearly there, but sometimes we don't notice them until 'wham!' they suddenly hit us and send us flying!"

Sarah also finds it fascinating that her mother had two wishes in life: to live in a glass house in the woods and to have an elephant. Recently, her family moved into a new house in the country—a secluded cottage down a dirt road. The house has many windows that look out into the woods. Miles loves going into his yard and feeding the chipmunks by hand. And, last year they took Miles to Lion Safari, a wildlife theme park where one of the key attractions is a baby elephant. To the amazement of the elephant's keeper, the young elephant, who normally shies away from people, walked right up to Miles. Miles now begs his parents to go back to the park to visit "his" elephant. Perhaps all of Margaret's wishes are now coming true.

## Blondie (Deb Wise)

Here is another case of an abusive mother who returns to her daughter. It is similar in a number of ways to the case of Sarah Holden, but it has a new twist. The mother in this case seems to have planned her rebirth to occur at a critical time in her daughter's life, providing the catalyst she needed to make a difficult decision and pull herself out of a dangerous marriage. I interpret it as the penitent mother's way of expressing her love and making up to her daughter for the pain she caused her before. If so, this is a marvelous example of a soul making amends to another soul by returning as its child.

When Deb Wise was nine, her family split up. Her father moved to another city in Canada two hours away and took Deb's four older siblings with him. Deb and her six-year-old sister stayed at home with their mother, Elizabeth. The breakup ruined Elizabeth. She was already addicted to prescription drugs, but now she fell into a deep depression and began to drink heavily.

Elizabeth turned into a monster when she drank. She verbally and physically abused both her young daughters. The father refused to return home because he couldn't handle his wife, so Deb and her sister were left alone to fend off their mother. The younger sister retreated to her bedroom, surviving as quietly as she could. Deb, on the other hand, was aggressive and lashed out at her mother, shielding her younger sister from their mother's frequent fits of temper. Sometimes in her sister's defense, Deb would push Elizabeth into the bedroom and lock her in. By the age of twelve, Deb remembers admitting to a friend that she sincerely hated her mother.

But over the years Elizabeth gradually mellowed, and when Deb was eighteen, she and her mother began to heal their relationship. Deb had broken up with her boyfriend of five years and was devastated. Her mother rallied with loving support during Deb's difficult time, becoming her best friend and confidante. Ironically, just as the mother-daughter bond they had both missed was blossoming, her mother suddenly lapsed into a coma and died two weeks later. Deb's younger sister, who was only sixteen at the time and badly damaged by their mother's abuse, didn't even cry when she died. But Deb grieved deeply for the newfound loving relationship with her mother that had ended so abruptly and for the healing that had been so suddenly interrupted.

Deb longed for her mother. Every night, for months after her death, she sat on the edge of her bed, addressed Elizabeth in the spirit world, and invited her to visit her, saying, "I'm not afraid of your coming back as a ghost. Please come back and see me." Deb would stare into her mirror and pray for her mother to appear. As far as she could tell, her prayers went unanswered.

She got married a few years later and started having children. The marriage proved to be a big mistake. Her husband frequently went on destructive drinking binges. During these times, Deb would have recurring dreams of Elizabeth. They were dreams of the happiest times in Deb's childhood, when she and her mother were together vacationing at their cottage on a lake.

These pleasant dreams were so vivid that when she awoke, Deb believed her mother had actually visited her, and the dreams left her feeling peaceful and happy.

But when she became pregnant again, the dreams stopped. The pregnancy, her fourth, was an accident— at least from Deb's point of view. She had finally separated from her abusive husband but didn't have the courage to end the marriage. In the meantime, she had fallen in love with Dennis, and the baby was his.

Dennis and I sat down and discussed our options. We were in absolute turmoil. We knew if we went ahead with having this child, we would bear the scorn of everyone in town. They would be frowning at us, to say the least, and make life hard for us for a long time. And I didn't know what it would do to my chances for getting a divorce from my husband if he found out I was pregnant. He'd know it wasn't his child.

We decided I had to have an abortion. That tore me apart. My whole life I had firmly believed what the Church taught, that abortion was an act of murder, and here I was making an appointment for one. The old saying, "Don't judge anyone until you've walked in their shoes," was slapping me in the face.

Something else happened when I first found out I was pregnant. Dennis didn't share our secret with anyone—he had a lot to lose, too. But one morning when he went to work, he could see that his best friend, Tom, had been crying. When Dennis asked what was wrong, Tom told him the most amazing story—and Tom's a real straight, churchgoing type who doesn't make up things. He said he had been awake all night because he kept hearing a baby crying. It drove him nuts because he thought it was a sign that a child somewhere was in

trouble. Dennis knew immediately what was going on.
He broke down and cried and told Tom the whole
story—he told him our secret. They both cried and Tom
begged Dennis to keep the baby no matter what we had
to go through to let it live. Dennis called me right away
and told me what Tom had said. We agreed to go ahead
with the pregnancy, knowing that many people would
be very unhappy with us and make our lives miserable.
But, we believed, God would be happy with us.

We were right about being scorned by the people in
our town, and even my family. So many people, even
my friends, completely turned their backs on me when
they could see I was pregnant. There were times when
I felt my new baby was my only connection to love because everyone else shunned me. They say babies can
feel everything. If that's true, this baby went through
a lot of rejection. With my other three pregnancies, I
was very excited and at peace and couldn't wait for
the baby. But with this one, I was filled with anxiety
and upset all the time.

My pregnancy pushed me to get the divorce. I know
if I hadn't become pregnant, I never would have had
the courage to stand up to my husband, who had cried
and begged on his knees for me to stay when I tried to
leave him before. I got my divorce, and Dennis and I
got married.

The baby was born in February 1993, and Deb
and Dennis named her Katie. She was a healthy, happy
baby who gave her family great joy. With a new baby
and a new husband who was kind to her and her children, Deb felt her life was finally turning a corner.

Katie was an early talker. As soon as she could
form full sentences, she repeatedly asked Deb, "Re-

member when I was your mummy?" Deb was amused
by Katie's remarks but didn't take them seriously.
After all, she thought, children say funny things like
that all of the time. Deb mentioned these remarks to
her sister on the phone, and they both had a good
laugh. But something happened when Katie was three
that convinced Deb that her daughter's remarks were
*not* a joke.

One evening, when Katie was not yet three, she and I
were waiting for my older daughter to finish her
horseback-riding lesson. We were lounging on some
hay in the barn when Katie leaned over and whispered
in my ear, "Do you remember when I was your
mummy?"

I'd heard her say this so many times by now and had
brushed it off. But this time I wasn't in a rush, so I humored her and played along. "No, tell me about it.
What was your name when you were my mummy?"

Whenever Katie has anything very special to say,
she always comes up close and whispers it to me. She
crawled into my lap, put her little hands on my cheeks,
looked at me with such a serious expression in her big
blue eyes, and whispered, "They used to call me
Blondie."

I was so startled, I almost knocked her off my lap. I
could feel the blood draining out of my face. I managed somehow to stutter, "They used to call you
Blondie?"

She answered, "Yes. Everybody called me Blondie
before."

Then I asked, "And I was *your* little girl?"

Again, she answered, "Yes."

I was shocked, because I knew my mother's nickname had been Blondie when she was younger, but nobody had called her that for years, and my children had never, ever heard us refer to her by that name. We always called her Elizabeth. I remembered that my aunts and uncles had called her "Aunt Blondie" around my cousins, but Katie had never met any of them.

Then Katie leaned toward me again and whispered in my ear in a very serious tone, "But I didn't like you very much when you were my little girl."

This hit me right in the gut. I offered, "Why didn't you? Mommies *always* love their little girls!"

She said, "Because you always used to yell at me, and push me into my room and lock the door."

I was speechless. When my mother got drunk, I would yell at her, pick her up and throw her back into bed, and lock her in her room until she sobered up. But no one—*no one*—but my sister, my mother, and I knew this. We never told anyone because we were afraid Children's Aid would take us away to foster homes and separate us. We hadn't talked about it since my mother died because we wanted to forget it. And Katie had *never* seen anything like this in our own house. I couldn't imagine how she would even know that it was possible for anyone to yell at their mother, let alone push her around.

## Another Kick at the Cat

After the incident in the barn, Katie rarely talked about her past life. But occasionally she would show unusual behaviors and tastes that mimicked Elizabeth and convinced Deb they were signs of who she was.

Early one morning I was busy in the kitchen making school lunches. Four-year-old Katie came in behind me and gave me a big hug. I still had my back turned to her when I heard her say, very matter-of-factly, "Do you know, Mummy, that one of my legs is bigger than the other?"

Again I had that feeling of the blood draining from my face, but I continued making sandwiches, trying not to betray my surprise. I questioned Katie calmly, "Oh, what do you mean? One leg is fatter than the other?" I was praying that was what she meant.

When I turned around to look at Katie, I saw the child sitting on the floor with her legs stretched out in front of her, and she was pointing to one of her legs to explain, "No, this one is longer than that one." I was shocked because my mother had often gone through the identical demonstration—but in a malicious way. She would sit on the floor with her legs stretched out before her and point out that one leg was longer than the other. She blamed the abnormality on having so many children, implying that we were to blame for wrecking her body. Here it was again coming from Katie, but this time with innocence.

Katie has bizarre preferences for foods that I think point unmistakably to her past life as my mother. She's really into butter. When we were away on holidays last week, one of my nieces commented that Katie likes her butter better than her bread. My sister and I used to tease my mother all the time because she would put six centimeters of butter on her bread—just like Katie does now.

When she was four, another odd preference for food popped out. Katie went to the fridge and got out the ketchup and bread and made herself a ketchup sandwich—just ketchup—without the hot dogs or baloney my kids usually ate. Katie thought this was the greatest thing she had ever tasted and was proud of herself, as if she had just invented it. Her sister and brothers thought this was hysterical—they had never seen or heard of such a thing! Until that moment I had completely forgotten ketchup sandwiches had been my mother's favorite snack. When we were growing up, we thought it was funny that my mother ate them, because just the thought of eating a ketchup sandwich made us gag. We later learned her love of these sandwiches was a carryover from the days of the Depression when she and her siblings sometimes had nothing else to eat. Now ketchup sandwiches are still Katie's favorite snack.

Deb explained how her experience with her daughter affected her outlook on life.

Christianity tries to tell us there is no such thing as reincarnation. I've never said "no, there isn't," or "yes, there is." But I have to say that after my experiences with Katie, I'm certainly leaning toward, "yes, there must be!" I think we keep coming back until we learn whatever the heck it is we're supposed to learn. I feel sad for my mother—she had a miserable childhood, and because of her addictions, she never had a good relationship with any of us. What a wasted life. Now, I feel if Katie is my mom, she gets another kick at the cat. Maybe this is her second, third, or hundredth life to try to figure it out. I think that's why she's back. Hopefully, this time things will be better. No matter who this soul is, I love her.

One thing I do know for sure: If Katie is my mom,

she saved my life. By coming back when she did, she forced me to get out of a bad and dangerous marriage. Maybe that was her way of repaying me for all of the mean things she did when I was growing up. And Katie's little signs, her telltale behaviors, I believe, are her way of letting me know she's back and that we can get on with having a loving relationship this time.

And one more thing. When Katie was four she said something amazing that convinced me she had planned her return, and that the timing was critical. I was preparing to go into town and I asked Katie if she wanted to go see Daddy at work and take him lunch. She said, "Is Uncle Tom going to be there?" [Tom was the best friend who convinced Deb and Dennis not to have the abortion.]

I said, "Yup, he is."

She came up close like she does when she has something important to say, and with a serious expression on her face, she whispered in my ear, "He saved my life once."

I was dumbfounded. I got goose bumps all over. I know it was her soul telling me *she knew*.

# Chapter 6

## *Choosing a Life*

*"When you go to heaven you have a little time to rest, kind of like a vacation, but then you have to get to work,"* four-year-old Courtney announced one day. *"You have to start thinking about what you have to learn in your next life. You have to start picking out your next family. Heaven isn't just a place to hang around forever. It's not just a place to relax and kick back. You have work to do there."*

When I was a young child, I believed that when a baby was born, a wise and skillful stork dropped it down the chimney of the expectant family's house. Pictures in my storybooks of storks donning blue vests and delivery hats, flying high above the chimney tops carrying babies in neatly tied bundles in their beaks, reinforced this idea. Since Santa Claus used the same method of delivery for his Christmas delights, it was not too far-fetched—I must have reasoned that all good things came down chimneys. This explanation was a little troubling, though, if I thought about all of those unfortunate families who might not have fireplaces and chimneys.

As I grew older, my childish notions gave way to my understanding of the scientific fact that babies are born out of the wombs of their mothers. Around the age of nine I was given a book called *From Little Acorns* that delicately described the process of reproduction in a 1950s kind of way. This book explained much more than I wanted to know about human biology, but still left the mystery: *why* are we born to one family instead of another? I drew on my religious training of an all-knowing, powerful, and arbitrary God to try to fill this gaping hole in my understanding. I imagined God in his cloudy heaven referring to a master list as he assigned parents to babies who were queuing up, waiting to be born. I concluded that where we are born is a matter of luck fated by an omniscient God. God decides. There was nothing in my religious training or in the culture around me to say otherwise. But if I thought about this explanation too much, I still felt uneasy. I couldn't understand why God chooses to give some children good homes, while other unfortunate ones are doomed to die in wars or of starvation. I knew there was something missing in this scheme too.

Many years later I'm still fascinated by the question of how our next life is decided. But now it's a serious question, central to my specialty, children's past life memories and same-family reincarnation. I've spent a lot of time exploring the idea, and the more I learn, the more I'm convinced—contrary to the common assumption—that there *are* things we can know about how we choose our next life. It's not an impenetrable mystery.

The question of choice is critically important to same-family reincarnation. Many people, even some who believe in reincarnation, assume we have no choice in deciding our next incarnation, and this belief prevents them from accepting the possibility of same-family reincarnation. They assume the distribution of souls is a random process or, at best, a process ruled by the natural laws of karma or the whims of a divine being. Therefore, they have trouble accepting same-family reincarnation because if the soul has no choice, the chances of a soul returning to the same family are millions to one, virtually impossible.

But in my research I have come across hundreds of cases of family return, similar to the ones you have read so far. It stands to reason we wouldn't be seeing *any* same-family cases if souls had no choice. The very existence of these cases of same-family reincarnation attests to the fact that there must be *some* choice, some intention, at least for *some* souls. Reincarnation is not a totally random process.

Another indication that the soul has choice comes from the statements of children themselves. Some children retain clear memories of their existence in the interlife state and of the journey leading to their birth, and they surprise their parents when they start talking about "before I was born." The parents take notice because these statements are different from what the children hear in Sunday school or from a storybook. They are often much different from the parents' own beliefs about heaven and existence before birth. Yet because the children speak about their sojourns in heaven so longingly, with such conviction and innocent wonder, the parents know the children are not making it up.

Over the years I've collected dozens of these cases

of children who speak of choosing their parents. From my interviews I have learned that these statements pop up unexpectedly, usually in a relaxed moment, while the child is getting ready for bed, riding in the car, or cuddling with Mommy or Daddy. Commonly the memories come out in snippets, a flash of story, a moment that the parents could easily have missed if they hadn't been alert. Often the child isn't even aware he or she is saying anything unusual. To them, it's just "something that happened." Each story has a slightly different twist, and the details vary. But they all agree on the bigger points, and the overall picture we get from putting together these many snippets from young children is the same. The common theme is that the soul participates in the process of choosing the next life.

## Mapping the Undiscovered Country

The picture of heaven we get from the children is reinforced by an entirely different source: past life therapy. Since the early 1960s thousands of people have reexperienced their past lives while under hypnosis and guided by a trained past life therapist. Past life therapy can be a powerful technique for resolving lifelong emotional and physical problems—sometimes very quickly.

Yet people who have never experienced a past life regression often assume it's *only* about past lives—about seeing yourself as a peasant in Germany or a slave in Egypt, for example. What they don't know is that through past life regression you can also experience, in full Technicolor, with Surround Sound realism, the mystical moment of death and what happens *after* leaving the body. At the moment of death, regression clients make a dramatic shift to a state of heightened awareness. From the vantage of their eternal soul, they gain tremendous insight into the life they just left behind and the issues their soul carries from lifetime to lifetime. Past life therapists know this after-death perception is often the source of the most profound revelations and healing.

With encouragement from their therapist guide, clients keep going forward beyond the moment of death to reexperience the life-review, planning and choosing the next life, and the return to a new body. In the process, they gain deep understanding of the spiritual reasons for choosing that particular life. And no matter how otherworldly the interlife experience is, when the session is over they can remember everything and describe (within the limits of language) what they saw. The understanding stays with them and often leads to profound adjustments in their lives. Some lose their fear of death.

In the course of conducting hundreds of these past life regressions, therapists noticed recurring patterns in what their clients experienced. A few therapists published studies and books describing what appeared to be true for all souls in the interlife process. These reports from therapists are valuable to corroborate and enhance what we hear in the reports from children. Because adults under hypnosis reveal much more detail than children's snippets of memory, the regression studies help us to complete the picture of the interlife and answer some questions of why and how we choose our next life. Most important, we see that adults and children agree on the main points—

particularly on the basic fact that the soul does have choice in deciding its next life.

In 1979 Dr. Helen Wambach, a seasoned past life therapist and researcher, was first to publish accounts of the interlife state. In her book *Life Before Life*, she describes her systematic exploration of the time before conception and birth. She designed experiments in which groups of several dozen people were hypnotized and regressed at the same time. Immediately afterward she asked them to write the answers to a series of questions about their prebirth memories, such as: Did you choose to be born? How did you feel about beginning your next life? Did you know your present mother before? What happened after conception? She compiled and analyzed the data from 750 regressions to build a conceptual model of the planning process before birth.

While Dr. Wambach was busy on the West Coast of the United States, Dr. Joel Whitton, a Canadian psychiatrist, was quietly collecting similar data from his past life therapy clients in Toronto, which he published in 1984 as *Life Between Life*. Not far behind Drs. Wambach and Whitton was another hypnotherapist researcher, Dr. Michael Newton of California, who published *Journey of Souls* in 1994, the culmination of twenty years of testimony from his clients. Compared with the other researchers, Dr. Newton paints a picture of highly structured interlife realms, with discrete levels of advancement and a multidimensional hierarchy of spirit helpers and guides. Despite the different flavor of Dr. Newton's version, the purpose behind all the heavenly activities reported by the three researchers is the same: All souls are intent on planning their next incarnation based on lessons they derive from the last one.

The findings of past life researchers are cross-validated by research on near-death experiences, or NDEs. NDEs are remarkably similar, point by point, to what clients see when they reexperience past life deaths through hypnosis. In the twenty-five years since the publication of Raymond Moody's pioneering work, *Life After Life,* researchers have documented thousands of cases of people who were clinically dead but revived and came back to report what they saw. Of course the accounts from NDEs go only so far—the experiencer returns to his body and lives to tell about it. But they add mightily to the consensus for what happens in the first stages of the journey.

Another validating source for what happens in the interlife state is the ancient writings of the Tibetan Buddhists. No discussion of these mystical realms can be complete without including their observations because, for more than twelve centuries, penetrating the interlife state has been a central part of their spiritual teaching. Their descriptions of the journey from death to birth have a lot in common with the accounts from NDEs and past life regressionists, especially around the moment of death. Plus, the Tibetans' poetic descriptions of the realms on the other side are unsurpassed in their vividness and beauty. They are useful in helping Westerners visualize these ineffable cosmic dimensions.

Drawing from the observations of all these varied sources, I've put together a composite sketch of the full journey in the afterlife, paying special attention to how we choose our lives. Overall, I believe this tour of heaven shows that what was once deemed impossible to fathom, the "undiscovered country," is indeed possible to know, or at least peek into. Although there is a lot our mortal brains will never comprehend, we can see enough to conclude that souls do have some degree of choice in where and when they reincarnate. When we look at the factors that influence a soul's decision, it becomes clear that choosing to continue a relationship within the same family is not only possible, it is sometimes the most logical and natural choice.

## A Tour Through Heaven

At the moment of death, accounts from all sources describe souls floating up and away from the body. No matter how wonderful or difficult was the life just ended, or how prolonged, sudden, or painful the death, souls feel a joyous release when they leave the body behind. They feel lighter, euphoric. Their senses become acutely alive as they step from the familiar three-dimensional, solid reality into a multidimensional realm of pure, vibrating energy, suffused with unearthly sights and sounds. All is energy and light. *The Tibetan Book of Living and Dying* describes this as an "all-pervasive landscape of light, brilliantly clear and radiant, transparent and multicolored, unlimited by any kind of dimension or direction—shimmering and constantly in motion."

Some people describe going through a tunnel, heading toward a light. Some don't. Whether they see a tunnel or not, most encounter a bright light and float toward it. They sense the radiant light as a conscious being of infinite intelligence who greets the disembodied traveler, embracing him in love and understanding that surpasses all worldly experience. It feels like a big welcome-home hug after a long trip.

The transition in consciousness at the moment of death can be confusing to some souls, especially if their deaths were sudden or traumatic. No matter. One or many luminous beings, who radiate boundless compassion, appear to orient the incoming soul to the eternal world of spirit: These guides may appear in the guise of a departed relative or friend, or religious personages that fulfill the traveler's expectations: Jesus, God, Buddha, nature spirits, deities, patriarchs, or saints. All communication between the guides and the incoming soul is telepathic and swift—they intuitively know *everything* about the soul and have been anticipating its arrival.

Children seldom remember this early phase of the after-death experience. But when they do, they also describe floating toward a light or going through a tunnel. They too report the presence of all-knowing and kind spirit beings whom they describe as mother and father figures, or God or Jesus. A five-year-old told her mother, "When you die you get sucked up to heaven by a light, and then you get to be whatever you want to be. But you don't talk in words. God doesn't use words like English or Spanish. He hears thoughts."

A father from England e-mailed about his three-year-old daughter, who spontaneously remembered going through the tunnel after dying.

One day, quite out of the blue, Karen told us she was waiting at a bus stop with her mummy when a car hit her and "took her to heaven." She said she went through a long tunnel and then she met God. She said she was "being lonely" and missed us, so she decided to come down to be our daughter and we gave her toys in her cot.

Whilst we are a Catholic family, we have not yet discussed religion with her or in front of her. We can accept that she would understand God and possibly heaven, but not about going "through a tunnel" or reincarnation.

On several occasions we discussed it with her further. Her facts remained unchanged, and if we pressed her for details that she didn't know, she would either say she didn't know, clam up, or make up something. In the latter case, we could clearly differentiate between the fact and fiction by the obvious change in her tone and manner.

A four-year-old boy remembered the odd fact that some souls don't know they're dead. One day when he and his father were discussing how far back he could remember, he surprised his father by announcing, "I remember when I was in heaven. I helped the dead guys." When his father asked him what he helped them do, the boy said, "Ya know, sometimes when people die they don't know they're dead, like when they die in car wrecks or real fast, they don't know they're dead. So we had to be there and wait until their soul left their body so we could help them get to heaven." Then he just smiled and ran off to play.

## Life Review

Four-year-old Courtney announced one day how busy she had been in heaven:

When you go to heaven, you have a little time to rest, kind of like a vacation, but then you have to get to

work. You have to start thinking about what you have
to learn in your next life. You have to start *picking out
your next family*, one that will help you learn whatever
it is you need to learn next. Heaven isn't just a place
to hang around forever. It's not just a place to relax
and kick back. You have work to do there.

Courtney's words are echoed by adults and others
who remember heaven. Heaven is not, as we are sometimes promised, a big resort in the clouds, a retirement
and a restful reward for enduring the hardships of an
earthly life. Yes, there is a period of rest, but then the
soul gets on with the job of learning and planning, and
even joins in to help with the business of heaven.

The first job in the planning process is to review and
evaluate the last incarnation. Some people report that,
with the help of guides, the soul steps into something
like a 3-D wraparound movie or holographic vision of
the life just left behind. Each moment in that life is re-
lived in full sensory detail. Everything is revealed. The
soul instantly senses the intentions behind every former action and feels with full emotional force the effects it had on others. These frank insights can be
joyous, sad, painful—but they are always enlightening.
Selfish and thoughtless acts are reexperienced with an-
guish and regret. Some souls feel great remorse for un-
fulfilled dreams, for not accomplishing what they set
out to do in that lifetime.

Throughout this review process, the soul observes
and judges its own actions and intentions. The guides
never judge or condemn. They stand by with ready
support as the soul goes through its emotional contor-
tions and is turned inside out for its own inspection.
They may help by tempering a soul's excessive self-

judgment, showing the soul its successes and failures in the broader context of its performance over many lifetimes.

*The Tibetan Book of the Dead* also describes the review process that occurs soon after death. It says that at the moment when we drop our physical bodies, the soul gains powers of clairvoyance and understands everything about the last life. The Lord of Death holds up the "Mirror of Karma," where all deeds of the past life are faithfully reflected and revisited in minute detail. Even "places where we did no more than spit on the ground" come back with a full force of memory and consciousness, and we reexperience the emotions and intention of each of our actions. They concur that "All judgment takes place in the mind: we are both judge and judged."[1]

## Why Souls Return

Clearly, there is a moral intelligence behind this life-review process. But the high moral standard is not imposed by the judgment of the guides or any other external authority. It is self-imposed. The soul employs its innate sense of right and wrong to evaluate its past performance.

The embodiment and expression of a moral standard appears to be the driving force behind reincarnation as the soul strives to become a truly loving, compassionate being. Exercising its free will, the soul may make long strides toward its goal in one lifetime, and trip and fall flat on its face in the next, hurting both itself and others.

The beauty of this process is that it is self-correcting.

Each incarnation offers us an opportunity to improve on our mistakes, *no matter how grievous,* rather than being eternally condemned for them. Reincarnation is the great equalizer. By changing bodies and life situations, we are given countless chances to shift perspective. We have infinite opportunities to truly understand whatever it is we need to learn about the human condition from all possible points of view. If we faced challenges that ended in failure last time, we have another go at it. For most of us, these lessons are not quickly or easily learned. It takes lifetimes.

My favorite metaphor for picturing the purpose of reincarnation comes from Rabbi Omer-Man as he explains to the Dalai Lama the Jewish concept of rebirth (quoted in the wonderful book *The Jew in the Lotus*):

> Each soul has to create a garment of light. In each incarnation . . . we make a little more or we undo a little according to our actions. In some incarnations, we do more damage, we pull out more threads; in other incarnations we weave more threads in. Ultimately the goal is to complete the garment.

As I see this image, when the garment of light is finally complete, we are light beings at one with God.

To amend past actions, to improve one's character, or to practice being more loving can be accomplished only while incarnate in a human body. The path to enlightenment runs through Earth, and the soul knows this. The objective of the life-review and planning process, then, is to choose an incarnation with the right measure of challenges and opportunities for learning and development.

The first decision is whether or not to reincarnate at

all. It's not a given that every soul has to return to
Earth, at least not right away. In Dr. Wambach's sample of 750 clients, 81 percent said they remembered
choosing between being born or remaining disincar-
nate. Even though they chose to be reborn, most approached the coming life with reluctance. They saw it
more as a duty, something unpleasant they had to do
for their spiritual development, like "washing the floor
when it's dirty" or "forcing yourself to jump into a
pool." It is not difficult to imagine how a soul would be
reluctant to leave a place of unconditional love and
supreme beauty to return to an imperfect world full of
struggle and pain. But the soul's desire for enlightenment, it's yearning to be in union with God, is stronger
than any hardships on Earth.

If the soul has reviewed and understands its own
spiritual needs and goals for the moment, and the decision is made to return to Earth, it is ready to enter the
planning stage for its next incarnation. It's time to
choose a life.

## Planning a Life

All the regression studies agree that the planning
process is done in collaboration with the spiritual
guides. The guides present the soul with options for the
next life. The soul's previous actions, or karma, determine the parameters and limits of its options. Based on
its past performance, the soul is offered a menu of lives
that will teach it what it needs to learn next. It does not
have *unlimited* choice. If that were the case, why
would anyone choose a life of hardship or tragedy?

Even with karma limiting the options, the soul still

has a mind-boggling number of lives to choose from. The coordination it requires to choose the right one is complex, a matter of balancing multidimensional factors in intricate ways. The decision must consider not only the needs of the soul, but must also coordinate its choice with the needs and plans of other souls it expects to join—particularly the parents. Although it is impossible with our finite comprehension to grasp all the variables that go into deciding one incarnation, we can talk about some of the more obvious ones.

First, there is the physical body to consider. We choose specific bodies for specific reasons. The case studies suggest that physical attributes are a part of the total package a soul selects to expedite whatever it needs to learn in the next life. Taking a handicapped body, for example, may accelerate the soul's advancement by giving it an opportunity to learn how to overcome obstacles or to concentrate on intellectual development. A strong male body may be what is required to learn about aggression or warfare. A beautiful body for either sex could force lessons in vanity and appearances. The choice involves balancing the desire to be with certain parents and whatever genetic package they offer with the need to have particular physical characteristics. Perhaps the soul can influence the forming body despite the genetic odds, as Dr. Stevenson's cases of birthmarks and birth defects suggest.

Relationships are vital to our learning and spiritual growth. So, arranging to reunite with certain souls in the coming life is a central element of the reincarnation plan. All the studies agree that we often reincarnate with souls we have been close to in other lifetimes. We may choose to return to those who nurtured and supported our growth in the past. To learn forgiveness, we may elect to return to someone who hurt us or did us wrong. Or the other way around: We may return to someone *we* wronged in order to make things right and pay a karmic debt.

Because relationships are so important, and because family relationships are so intense, it makes sense that a soul would have many, many reasons to return to the family it just left. This is why, I believe, same-family reincarnation is so common.

The selection of parents is the most critical decision in the planning process because it sets the stage for the coming lifetime. It's no wonder young children seem to remember choosing their parents more than any other aspect of their prebirth experience. They often tell their parents why they chose them, claiming either that it was their decision alone or one that was made with the help of guides.

## Choosing Parents

It is common for children to say how excited they were when they chose their parents. Since I hear this so often, I suspect that parents must hear it all the time. But many parents miss the opportunity to learn why they were chosen because they brush off their children's remarks as an active imagination or cuteness.

Jessa's parents, however, could not miss her statements. She talked about heaven constantly:

> We are not a religious family, but since the age of two, Jessa would tell us stories about God. She said that before she was born, she was God's daughter and she sat

by God. She said before she was born, she picked us as parents because we needed someone like her in our lives!

She said before she was God's daughter, she had other parents, Michael and Susan, who were killed in a fire. She described a small wooden house. She talks endlessly about death and how we shouldn't be scared. She tells us not to be sad about her grandparents who died recently because they are in a beautiful serene place now.

The following story is the pure recollection of one contrite soul who is now in the body of a three-year-old. It is a poignant example of a soul who came back to make up for a wrong she inflicted years ago. Her mother, Carrie, described to me in a telephone interview what happened:

I was sitting on the couch reading when Amanda walked up and said, quite out of the blue, "Mommy, remember a long, long time ago—before you were born?"

I put my book down and gave Amanda my full attention. "No," I said.

She lay down on her stomach on the coffee table, tilted her head, and looked at me. With the most serious tone she informed me, "I killed you!" Just as matter-of-fact as can be.

Without expressing surprise or disbelief, I asked, "You did? Why?"

She said, "I was so mad at you." She got a really sad look on her face and moved onto the couch and cuddled up.

I asked, "How did you kill me?"

"With a shotgun."

I wasn't expecting that! I was curious how she felt about all of this and asked, "Well, if that's what happened, what are we doing now?"

Her response chilled me. "Mama, I was so sad for you. I wanted to be your friend again. I'll never do that again. I just want to be in your family now." I realized she had tried to tell me the same thing a few nights before.

We have a phenomenal relationship. We are very, very close. But now that I'm thinking about it, I remember a number of occasions when Amanda had no reason to be sad, but she said, "I'm very sad for you. Let me hold your hand." Now that she's confessed to murdering me in a past life, I can see how all the pieces go together. I believe she's been trying to make up to me all along and tell me how sorry she is. It's clear now. She really is upset about what she did!

I remember reading in *Children's Past Lives* where you said parents could help a child come to terms with a past life memory. I reread parts of it and understood what I had to do. A few nights later, when we were relaxing before bedtime, I said as casually as I could, "Amanda, do you remember before *I* was born?"

She said, "Yes, but I don't want to talk about it. I was a very, very bad man. And it makes me very sad."

I reassured her: "Amanda, if that makes you sad, it's okay. I just want you to understand that I forgive you for whatever happened and we're now in a different life. I love you very much and you're my daughter now."

She wrapped her arms around me and said, "Mommy, I love you so much."

Her big blue eyes looked deep into mine, telling me she understood. And that was it. She changed the subject. But I was sitting there, totally stunned. Immediately I knew what she had said was true. Strangely enough, I have always believed I was murdered in a past life, but I never mentioned this to her or to anyone else.

And that was the last time she said anything about being sad for me.

## Good Plans, Bad Plans, No Plans

Not all souls participate equally in the planning process. Some are actively involved and choose carefully; others are passive, drifting into their next lives without much preparation. Some apparently never leave the earth vibration and wander aimlessly until they fall into a convenient womb. It's not a tidy process, not uniform or predictable, follows no formulas, and is definitely not the same for every soul.

A good analogy to this is teenagers picking a college. Some invest themselves fully in the decision. They begin planning well in advance, study hard to make the grade for a good school, and research dozens of colleges and universities to select the one that best fits their needs. On the other hand, some students are passive and don't give college any thought until the last minute. They end up attending the school down the road or the one their parents picked for them. Or sometimes they pick a school for trivial reasons—because their boyfriend goes there or the school's football team made it to the playoffs last year. Most students fall somewhere in between these two extremes. The degree of planning souls do when choosing a life varies in much the same way.

It seems that in choosing a life the difference in the degree of planning is dependent on the soul's maturity and awareness. Studies agree that advanced souls spend more time in the afterlife learning and weighing plans for their next incarnation than less mature souls do. Since the advanced souls have mastered a higher level of lessons and skills on Earth, they have the understanding to create more ambitious and finely tuned plans. On the other hand, less advanced, "beginner" souls rush through the interlife without giving much thought to what they are doing and jump back into the first body that seems good enough. These lives have a smaller chance of being productive compared with those that are carefully planned. The unplanned lives are more likely to end up being drab and meaningless or chaotic, or the individual may be overwhelmed by challenges it is not equipped to handle.

The Tibetan Buddhists agree that the more aware and conscious a soul is, the better its choices will be for the coming life. They say a spiritually evolved soul can direct its incarnation and choose the place and family of its rebirth. Otherwise, they say, karma will dictate the choice, and the soul will be drawn, as to a magnet, into whatever womb resonates with all its past experiences. They advise the traveler scanning the landscape for its birth destination that the right place to be born will "shine most prominently, like a beacon."[2]

Only 26 percent of Dr. Wambach's respondents felt they had planned their lifetimes carefully and were eager to get started. They added that they were confident their spiritual guides would continue to help them with inner guidance when they needed it during the next life. The majority of respondents, though, were not as confident or excited. They didn't desire to be born and resisted the birth experience. These souls were far too comfortable in the interlife state and simply didn't want to leave. One observed, "Yes, I chose to be born, but I didn't arrange it. It was rather like a travel agent giving me a tour to go on." And then there are some—about 3 percent in Dr. Wambach's study—who reported going against the advice of their guides because they were impatient or impulsive and felt compelled to jump back into a body.[3]

## Pinkie Swear

A good friend of mine told me this story about her daughter and niece—cousins who are also inseparable friends. It suggests how strong the influence of the guides can be when determining the time and place of a soul's return.

Rebecca, our baby-sitter, came up from the beach of our summer home in Maine that we always share with my brother's family. She shook her head and announced, "Those girls are in a world of their own! The stories they're concocting just make me laugh. And since they've sworn me to pinkie swear secrecy, I can't even let you in on their tale!"

Rebecca was talking about my seven-year-old niece, Sarah, and my daughter, Charlotte, who's a year younger. I smiled as I contemplated the girls' latest creative moment. Even though they only saw each other two or three times a year, they were as thick as thieves and always up to much merrymaking. In fact, they were more like sisters than cousins and so psychically "in tune" they often kept their verbal communication with each other to a minimum.

Curious about their newest story and needing a break from my dishwashing, I dried my hands and walked down to the beach to find out exactly what they were up to. Between the last patch of purple lupine and the rocky shore, I found them dressed exactly alike in pretty pink dresses, pink headbands, and white sneakers. They were giggling about something.

"So, my little ones," I interrupted, "Rebecca said you two were creating some mighty fine tales. Perhaps you will share one with me because she said she pinkie swore and wouldn't tell me what you told her if her life depended on it!"

Upon hearing my request, the two girls froze. They stared at each other and after a slow minute came to a silent conclusion: Charlotte would be the one to speak.

She whispered, "Mom, this is a hard thing to say. I don't know if I can say it so you'll get it."

I whispered back, "Just try."

"Well, only Sarah and I, and now Rebecca, know this, so you have to promise not to tell anyone."

"Yeah," Sarah chimed in, "you've got to pinkie swear!"

With my left and right pinkies extended, I hooked up with theirs and swore myself to utter secrecy.

Content with our pact, Charlotte began, "Now, don't get upset, Mom, because this is kinda weird."

I nodded for her to continue.

"Before Sarah and I came here to this life, we were supposed to come together. We were twins and we were supposed to be in Tricia's [my sister-in-law's] stomach. Just before we came, that person held me back. Remember him, Sarah? Do you remember what he told me?"

Sarah nodded seriously and said, "He told you that you couldn't come. That it wasn't your time yet, but that he'd make it so we could always be near each other. He said you'd have to wait and we were so upset—but look! Here we are! He kept his promise!"

The girls hugged each other as I contemplated their short but amazing story. I knew enough about reincarnation—and their incredible bond—to accept the validity of their experience and the truth of their account. I thanked them. As I walked back up to the house I realized if I had not been receptive to their tale, I might have missed out on one of the most special "out of the mouths of babes" stories I'd ever heard.

## Hanging Out on the Earth Plane

Dr. Stevenson's findings are in basic agreement with the regression studies and the writings of Tibetan Buddhists. He has found evidence that some souls choose the circumstances of their next incarnation. He also agrees that choice ranges widely, from cases where souls choose for trivial reasons or no reason, to cases where there is clear evidence of volition. In some of his verified cases, the reasons for the choice can be discerned from examining the circumstances of the previous life.

His many same-family cases add weight to the conclusion that reincarnation is *not* random. He reasons that *something* drew the soul back into the family. Dr. Stevenson theorizes that love and familiarity create a bond—he calls it a "psychic force"—that acts as an attractor to help the discarnate personality find its way back to the family. There may be other attractors too: the need to finish a task, an affinity to a certain place, even an unpaid debt.

Some Stevenson cases offer examples of souls who do no planning whatsoever, which confirms what the past life therapists found. In these cases, after the person dies, the souls never leave the earth plane and remain in the vicinity of where they died. They hang out at the same location, sometimes for many years, and seem to be aware of the daily activities of people in the area. They may even try to interact with the locals, much as a ghost would. Until one day, the disembodied spirit spots a potential mother or father and is drawn to them, follows them home, and is reborn as their child. At first these cases sound too bizarre to be true—it's easy to think the child could be making it all up. But in each case, Dr. Stevenson corroborates the statements by confirming that just before the conception of that child, one of the parents had been in the area where the child claimed to have been "hanging out."

The next two cases from Dr. Stevenson's published works illustrate this surprising phenomenon.

A two-year-old boy from Thailand named Bongkuch told his parents his name was really Chamrat and he had lived in a town nine kilometers from where he presently lived. He said that when he was Chamrat he had been robbed and killed. After his death, he sat in a tree near the site of his murder for about seven years. One rainy day he saw his present father and followed him home on a bus. His father, a school principal, recalled that before his wife became pregnant with Bongkuch, he had attended a meeting in the town where his son claimed to have died. He also remembered that it had rained that day. Chamrat made many more detailed statements that confirmed he was remembering the life of a man who had been robbed and killed in that town.[4]

A Burmese child, U Tinn Sein, remembered being a Japanese soldier fighting in Burma during World War II. He had been shooting his rifle at a low-flying enemy plane when the plane's machine gun shot him in the chest. (U Tinn was born with a birthmark on his chest.) After dying, he remained in the area of a nearby pagoda and enjoyed throwing stones at passing bullock-carts. (According to Dr. Stevenson, rock throwing is not an unusual activity for discarnate beings.) One day he saw his father driving by in a bullock-cart, was attracted to him, and followed him home. The father confirmed that he had often gone to that area to collect firewood in the period before his son's conception.[5]

## Being Is Believing

Another intriguing pattern emerges from Dr. Stevenson's cases. Up to now we have been looking at how souls choose and plan their next incarnations while in heaven. But Dr. Stevenson has evidence that what we believe and intend *before* death can influence our next incarnation as well. This idea has enormous implications, both for us as individuals and for understanding the rebirth process in general.

Beliefs shared by members of a particular culture influence the reincarnation patterns within that culture. For example, in Burma and Thailand many believe it is possible to change sex in the next life—a male in one life reincarnates as a female in the next, and vice versa. Consequently, in these cultures Dr. Stevenson finds more than the usual number of what he calls sex-change cases. Other cultures—the Druse of Lebanon and the Tlingit of Alaska for example—do *not* believe that it is possible to change sex from one incarnation to the next, and few sex-change cases are found among these peoples. The Druse also believe that a person must reincarnate immediately, with no gap of even a minute between death and birth; many of Dr. Stevenson's cases in which the interval between death and birth is less than nine months are found among the Druse. Dr. Stevenson speculates that in cases like these, belief may act as something like a posthypnotic suggestion on the incarnating soul.[6]

Belief also influences the incidence of cases of reincarnation in the same family. In cultures that believe it is normal to return to the same family in the next life—the Burmese, the Igbo of Nigeria, the Gitksan of British Columbia, and the Tlingit of Alaska—same-family cases are the rule rather than the exception. In Sri Lanka, however, where it is not expected that a soul can return to the same family, almost no same-family cases are found.[7]

If belief and intention can affect broad patterns within a culture, can belief and intention also influence the outcome of individual reincarnations? Yes, they can.

It's true for the Tibetan Buddhists. They have a tradition in which their highest, most spiritually advanced teachers, or *lamas*, predict where they will be reborn. For centuries, the succession of Dali Lamas has been the supreme example of this. Before their deaths high lamas share their predictions, couched in symbolic im-

ages, with their disciples. A few years after their
deaths, the disciples use these clues to locate young
candidates, children from two to five years old, and put
each of them through tests of memory. The correct
child will have explicit and accurate memories of the
deceased lama's life. He will also prove to be a spiritual prodigy, able to instantly memorize and interpret
volumes of scripture and perform elaborate rituals
mastered in previous lives. The Buddhists believe that
only the spiritually adept, who are well practiced in the
esoteric teachings and disciplines, are able to direct
their own rebirths with such precision.

But Dr. Stevenson has found that the spiritually adept
are not the only ones who can predict and direct their
next incarnation. Some cultures, most notably the Tlingit of Alaska, take it for granted that any person can
choose and predict *before* dying where he will reincarnate. Dr. Stevenson presents a number of cases in which
an elderly person declares to a young female relative of
childbearing age that he wishes to be reborn to her. And,
judging from the evidence, this is exactly what happens.
A child born to that mother shows signs—statements,
behaviors, and birthmarks—of the deceased relative.

The case of Corliss Chotkin Jr., of the Tlingit of
Alaska, is an example of this.

A year before Victor Vincent died, he told his niece
Irene Chotkin that he hoped to reincarnate as her son.
He told her he thought she would be a good mother to
him, better than the other candidates in the family. He
also believed his beloved sister had already reincarnated as Irene's daughter, and he wanted to be with her
again. Victor told Irene she would recognize him by
looking for birthmarks that correspond to two surgical

scars he had and pointed them out to her—one near the bridge of his nose and the other on his upper back.

Eighteen months after Victor's death, Irene had a son she named Corliss. At his birth she noticed he had two birthmarks that corresponded exactly to the scars her uncle had shown her. When Corliss was just learning to talk and Irene was trying to teach him to repeat his name, he insisted that his name was really "Kahkody," which was Victor Vincent's tribal name. When Corliss was two years old, he spontaneously recognized several people from Victor's life, including his widow, and he accurately remembered events from Victor's life that no one had ever mentioned. Corliss also showed behaviors that resembled Victor's. At a very early age he had a precocious ability to fix engines, which is what Victor had done for a living. Because of all these signs, the family believed Victor's prediction had come to pass and he was indeed reborn as their son.[8]

## The Angel of Forgetfulness

After going through the full process of planning, and choosing our lives, why don't more of us remember any of it? This is an ancient mystery, and different philosophical traditions through the centuries have created their own myths to explain why we forget.

In ancient Greece, Plato wrote that reincarnating souls drink water from the River of Forgetfulness, whose water "no pitcher may hold." Once the soul drinks this water, it forgets everything about the afterlife.[9]

A medieval Jewish text called the *Creation of the Universe* describes the gentle ministry of the Angel of Forgetfulness:

Finally, the time comes for the soul to enter the world. It is reluctant to leave, but the angel touches the baby on the nose, extinguishes the light above the head, and sends it forth into the world. Instantly, the soul forgets all that it has seen and learned and enters the world crying, having just lost a place of shelter, rest, and security.[10]

This Angel of Forgetfulness, according to other stories, touches us on the upper lip, making a little indentation, just before we are born. The angelic touch erases all memory of our heavenly home and the reasons we chose this life. This amnesia serves an important purpose. According to past life therapist Dr. Joel Whitton, it "allows the individual to embark on the new life unhindered by confusing echoes of past deeds and misdeeds. In souls who have experienced the light it also prevents pining and homesickness for the grandeur that has been left behind."[11]

Sometimes though, the amnesia isn't total, and some memories of heaven seep through. In the following story, one four-year-old boy remembered one key moment from the planning process for his life, which he shared with his father. Many years later this information helped his father deal with the grief of an unthinkable tragedy.

## Remembering the Plan

David Schultz was an internationally acclaimed wrestler, having won the U.S. Nationals four times and an Olympic gold medal in 1984. Because of his love for the sport and his zest for life, he was considered an ambassador of friendship to people all over the world who knew him. Even his opponents, especially the Russians, loved David as their friend.

On January, 26, 1996, David was murdered by John Du Pont, heir to the Du Pont fortune. John was the patron of a wrestling training center near Philadelphia where David trained for seven years.

Hundreds attended a memorial service for David in Philadelphia. His father, Philip, told this story in his eulogy. I heard later from a friend who was there that every person in the room listened in rapt silence as Philip told his story. Waves of emotion swept through the audience. No one was left unmoved.

Philip wrote out the full story for me so I could share it here:

> When my daughter-in-law called me at about three o'clock in the afternoon of the twenty-sixth to tell me David was dead, I broke down in shock and disbelief, sobbing out the predictable *whys*. Fortunately, a friend of mine was there to console me. In my anguish, I kept repeating the same questions. All I knew for sure was I had lost my son, the most precious soul I had ever known. He was more than my son; we were wonderful friends, as well.
>
> In the midst of this anguish, I suddenly remembered a story David shared with me when he was only four years old. I remembered that at the time when he shared this special vision with me, I was totally enveloped in his words, and in awe of how detailed and mature his account was.
>
> I never forgot that moment. And now, thirty-two years later, it has given much solace to me, all of David's family, and multitudes of friends. I am con-

vinced his story is absolutely true, and that I was meant to hear it, remember it, and tell it now, for it is redemptive, inspiring, awesome, and delightful.

Thirty-two years ago David and I were walking holding hands in a redwood grove near our house in California. I recall taking infinite pleasure in the moment we were having together. Every once in a while he almost stumbled, but he would just keep going, undaunted.

After he stumbled a second time, he held on to my hand tighter. Then he stopped and said with wide-eyed wonder and joy, "I've got a really, *really* big secret to tell you!"

"Oh, good!" I replied, savoring his enthusiasm and trust in me. "I *love* secrets."

"But," he added, with a note of warning in his voice, "you must promise you won't tell anyone." I promised. "And you can't laugh at me."

"I'd never laugh at you. Ever! Ever!" I didn't want to interrupt his special moment.

"Because"—and David became quite serious— "this happened before I was born, and it was up in the sky—way up in the clouds."

I remember catching my breath when he told me this. I'm sure my mouth was wide open in total wonderment and expectation. "Well, sweetheart, what happened?"

"Well, you see, there were these twelve men."

"Twelve men?" I asked incredulously. "You actually counted them? One-two-three-four and so on?"

David nodded. "Uh-huh, twelve. I counted them." At that moment he seemed quite a bit older than his four years. He continued, his eyes gleaming with joy: "And they were in a circle. Like they were sitting around a cloud or a table, but I didn't see any table. I could see they had faces, but they didn't have bodies."

David just kept looking at me with a kind of Cheshire-like smile. "Well, what happened, David? Tell me, I can hardly stand it."

"Well"—he sort of sucked in his cheeks—"well, one of them spoke. Nobody else said anything. And they all looked kind of old. But the man who spoke to me looked like he was the oldest."

"And what did he say?"

"Oh, he told me I had to go down there." He pointed with his finger, indicating that down there was on the earth. He continued, "Down there—way down there I had to go to be tested." He repeated himself, "I mean, I had to go down there to be tested."

"David, this story is so wonderful. But, I'm curious," I said as we walked under one of the biggest redwood trees. "Are you going to pass the test?"

David held my hand more easily now as we ambled along. He gave me a cheery smile. "Oh, yes!"

"Oh, good!" I replied, finally exhaling.

We walked a little farther in silence. Then he stopped and looked up at me, just beaming. "But I won't be here long."

And, at this point, he let go of my hand and went off to play by himself, leaving me to ponder this extraordinary parable. I never mentioned it again, as I promised. Until now.

Needless to say, this story has brought peace and a real sense of *knowing* around this senseless, stunning tragedy. And I'll never stop thanking David for sharing his story with me. Ever. Ever.

# Chapter 7

## U-turn in the Womb

*Then Sam jumped up on the bed and started counting on his fingers. "First I was in Aunt Molly's tummy and I didn't get born. Then I tried to get back into Aunt Molly's tummy, but Sophie was there in the way. So I tried to kick her out. Then I got in your tummy and then I got born." He paused and then said in all seriousness, "I sure did work hard getting here, Mom!"*

We all know what it's like to make plans to do something and then be forced to abandon those plans either because circumstances change or because we change our minds. Surprisingly, it appears that the same can happen to souls planning to be reborn. They sometimes have a change of plans and do a quick U-turn in the womb. And it can happen *anytime* during the nine months of pregnancy. It seems, from the evidence in the following stories, that plans for the coming lifetime are not fixed or irrevocable, even if they were carefully laid out in the period between lives.

From our ordinary, earth-bound perspective these changes of plan are called by the medical terms *miscarriage* and *stillbirth*. Most people, if they have never been through the experience, can't understand how deeply the parents feel a miscarriage or a stillbirth as a death, an inexplicable loss that leaves them bereft and grieving for a child they never knew. Their beautiful hopes and dreams for loving companionship with the new baby evaporate. Adding to the pain, no matter what the medical explanation is they inevitably blame themselves at some point, wondering what they did wrong.

Yet looking at miscarriages and stillbirths from the perspective of the incoming soul turns our thinking inside out. From the soul's perspective, a decision not to be born at a particular time and to a particular mother is simply a detour, a zigzag in the continuing journey through eons of lifetimes. Souls decide to switch course for any number of reasons: to change sex or birth order, to wait for a more appropriate body for the soul's purposes, to wait until the parents' circumstances improve, or to readjust the timing of a predestined rendezvous with another soul already on Earth or yet to incarnate. Or, it may be due to the biological fact that the fetus was defective.

Whatever the reason, it is clear that in some cases souls wait for another opportunity to return to the same family. How do we know? Because some children remember the whole process. Then one day, in the middle of a casual conversation, they tell their parents about it. They innocently describe earlier attempts to be born to the mother or through another woman in the extended family. The parents are always shocked at first if the child's claim corresponds exactly to a pregnancy loss that had been kept hushed up, a personal secret too painful to talk about, and something beyond the comprehension of such a very young child. But after absorbing the truth of what their child is telling them, their shock turns to joy and relief when they realize the baby who died in the womb years ago was not lost to them forever.

Seeing these events from the soul's timeless point of view makes it easier for the family to accept a pregnancy loss as the *soul's* choice not to come at that time—a choice independent of anything the parents did or didn't do. It gives the grieving parents solace and assuages their guilt.

The three cases that follow give a sample of how some parents encountered these memories in their children, and what it meant for them. The latter part of this chapter discusses abortion—a special case of an imposed detour—from the perspective of the indestructible soul and shows that these souls too can return to the same family.

## A Change of Plans

The first miscarriage case that caught my attention was told during a workshop I gave in San Francisco a few years ago. I had never before appreciated how profoundly healing it can be to know that a miscarried baby has returned to the family. The group was spellbound as therapist Carolene Heart told her story.

Brittany is my granddaughter. When she was three she called me on the telephone and left a message on my answering machine: "Meemaw, come! Mommy and I argued."

I called Karen, my daughter, and asked, "What's wrong? Brittany called and left a message on my machine."

Karen said, "Are you sure? How did she know your number?" So I played back the message for her. She laughed in disbelief, then told me to come right over.

When I got there, I asked Brittany, "What's the matter?"

She crawled into my lap and whimpered, "Mommy doesn't 'member."

"Mommy doesn't remember what?"

"Mommy doesn't 'member when I was in your tummy."

My daughter Karen, addressing me, said, "I've *tried* to explain to Brittany that I'm *your* daughter and she is *my* daughter and that she grew in *my* tummy, not yours."

Brittany listened patiently to her mother's explanation, and then asserted: "No, *before* that, when I was in Meemaw's tummy *with you*, Mommy. I couldn't stay because I didn't want to be a boy."

I got goose bumps all over my body. Karen ran from the room crying. We both knew that when I was pregnant with Karen, she had a twin brother who died at seven months in utero.

A few minutes later Karen came back, sniffling back her tears. She hugged Brittany, then she hugged me. She said, "This is so wonderful. I can't believe it. After all these years I'm back with my twin again."

## Light Friends

Here is another story of a change of plans that occurred more than midway through the pregnancy. This young child remembered terminating her first plan to be born. Interestingly, she was aware of the effect of her decision on her first choice of parents. Her story shows that the incoming soul is not insensitive to the emotional effects of its decision on others. Her mother, Naomi, tells what happened.

From the time Sarah was able to speak, and was still in her crib, she told me she missed her "light friends." As she got older, whenever she spoke of them she would get a distant, longing look on her face as she told me how she used to fly everywhere with her light friends before she was born. She was worried now that she had forgotten how to fly.

One day just before her nap, when she was three, Sarah and I were cuddling together. She looked me in the eye and said, very seriously, "I'm so glad Jesus helped me pick you and Daddy to be my parents."

I gasped in amazement and managed to blurt out, "What?"

Sarah went on: "I sat on His knee and we looked down at you and Daddy, *and two other people,* and I said I wanted you and Daddy and then we laughed and went to play." She added, *"I was supposed to be a boy, but changed my mind and then wanted to be a girl."*

For months after this, Sarah continued to speak of how she longed for heaven, and how she missed God and Jesus and "flying around with her light friends."

Sarah's parents, who weren't regular churchgoers and who didn't believe in reincarnation either, were baffled by their daughter's obsession with heaven. Yet Naomi wondered if Sarah's remark about originally intending to be a boy could explain why she was not a "ribbons and dresses" kind of girl. Sarah resisted wearing dresses and often told her parents that girls are boring. Instead, she wanted to wear her hair very short, preferred to play in the mud, and always asked for boys' toys. For Christmas, she asked for things like a racing car and *Star Wars* fighters—never a doll.

When she was four, her parents decided to move from their home in Jacksonville, Florida, to take a new job in Atlanta. Sarah suddenly became very upset about leaving her grandparents, who lived nearby. But it wasn't that she was sad about not being able to visit them herself. She was deeply concerned about how her *grandparents* would feel when she moved away. She cried over and over to her mother, "They will think I died." Naomi guessed this strange statement and Sarah's intense feelings were related to the recent death of her guinea pig—perhaps she equated her feelings of loss for her pet with the coming separation from her grandparents. Naomi did her best to calm Sarah by reminding her that after the move she would still see her grandparents often.

But then Sarah said something that changed their minds about her puzzling statements. Naomi continues:

> One night my husband, Orin, was putting Sarah into bed while I was reading in the next room. I could hear their conversation clearly, and when I heard her ask, "Daddy, how do God and Jesus make babies?" I stopped reading and listened.
>
> I smiled as I heard Orin stutter, caught off guard by this important question. Yet he managed to frame a careful answer for our four-year-old daughter. "Well, mommies and daddies make the baby and God sends the soul down from heaven."

Sarah paused and sighed.

He asked, "Are you thinking of when you were with God and Jesus and picked us as parents?"

"No, I didn't pick you as parents first. I picked *your* parents to be my mom and dad."

He corrected her, "You mean you picked them to be your *grand*parents."

"Nooo, Daddy, when they were younger, I was going to be their little boy before you came." This was new. I'd never heard Sarah say anything like this before. I moved to the door of the bedroom and leaned in.

Orin asked her, "Aren't they a little old to be your parents?"

She sighed again in exasperation. "Nooo, Daddy, when they were younger, I was going to be *their* little boy before *you* came. But I decided not to and left."

Seeing the stunned look on her father's face, she quickly added, "But it's okay. I really love you guys too. I'm okay with it." Orin was silent, unable to speak. Sarah asked, "Am I freaking you out, Daddy?"

He assured her he was fine and finished tucking her in. Then, just as suddenly as the conversation began, it changed, and Sarah was chatting happily about going to the beach the next day. We both kissed her good night and withdrew to the living room.

I asked my husband, "Did your mom ever have a miscarriage?"

He said, "No, not that I'm aware of." But the suspense was too much for him. Without saying another word, he picked up the phone and called Greg, his older brother by eight years.

"Did Mom ever have a miscarriage?" he asked into the phone.

During the long silence that followed, I watched Orin's face turn white.

He hung up the phone and said, "Yes, Mom had a pregnancy before she was pregnant with me. It was stillborn and it was a boy—just like Sarah said."

Orin was visibly shaken, and continued. "I never knew that before. Nobody ever mentioned it. The only reason Greg knew was because one day when he was little, he accidentally overheard Mom crying on the phone, whispering about the miscarriage with a girl-friend."

We stared at each other, speechless, as the realization sank in. If Sarah was right on this, maybe her other remarks about her light friends and picking us as parents were real memories, and not an active imagi-nation as we had supposed.

After telling me this story, Naomi added that this in-formation about the miscarriage cleared up another lit-tle mystery. When Sarah was two she couldn't understand the concept of parents/grandparents/aunts/uncles. She always insisted that Orin's parents were her parents. They all misinterpreted this "confusion" as a toddler's cuteness. Now they understood.

Sarah is now five, and she seems to have forgotten her confusion about nearly being born as a boy. Naomi reports that she is finally settling into "girl mode." She is playing with baby dolls for the very first time and re-cently asked for Barbie dolls for her birthday. She is also letting her hair grow out so she can put it in pony-tails.

## Cousins!

Souls sometimes travel in groups. The idea of soul mates is common in fiction as well as in serious books on reincarnation. But what happens when one of two souls with an implicit agreement to travel together exercises its free will and vetoes the plan for the next incarnation? Like any traveling companions who don't see eye to eye on the itinerary, quarrels ensue. This next story is an example of exactly that kind of disagreement. Notice how the quarrel between the two brothers, Sam and Peyton, affected Sam's personality until he finally came to accept his fate.

The story is condensed from the journals the mother, Jodie, kept as it was unfolding. Sam made many more statements not reported here in which he gave accurate details of his birth and at least two past lives, and he described "the other world" where he lived before he was born. He is one of those young children who have such clear prebirth memories that they can't understand when nobody else remembers, and are frustrated when none of the adults around them can answer their questions.

Sam's first word was *cousins*. I recorded this odd fact in his baby book under the entry: "first words." Now that I know the whole story, I understand why that word meant so much to him.

Sam was obsessed with his cousins since he was a baby. When we first took him from Sacramento to visit them in San Francisco, before he could talk, he was visibly changed from the moment he saw them, excited and happy to be with the four cousins and his aunt Molly and uncle David. But his continuing obsession didn't make a lot of sense because the cousins were much older than Sam—six to twelve years older—and we didn't visit them more than a couple of times a year. But every visit was a huge event for Sam. He *loved* being with that family.

David and Molly are the brother and sister-in-law of my husband, Michael. The first time we visited them, I noticed in their bedroom a little memorial they had for the twins Molly lost during pregnancy. But Michael warned me not to say anything about it. He said no one talks about it, it's too painful for them. She lost them at eight and a half months. We learned later that the umbilical cord that sustained both babies was defective and got kinked and both twins died. They would have been David and Molly's second and third children, after Kevin, who was the oldest; her other three children are girls.

Even though I didn't know Molly very well, I asked her to be with me at Sam's birth. I didn't know at the time why I asked her—I had other family who were closer. When I told her my due date, October 19, she responded, "Oh, my God, that's the day I lost the twins." She went out of her way to be at Sam's birth in 1994, and again at Peyton's birth in 1996. Even though Molly and I didn't see each other often, we became very close.

From the time Sam figured out that the car was the vehicle that would take him to his cousins' house, every time we got in the car he would yell, "Cousins! Cousins!" I would have to break the news to him that we were not going to the cousins' house, but we were going to the store or the library or the park. He would pitch a fit! It got so bad I actually avoided using the car if I could walk to where I was going. Every time we got in the car he would have a meltdown because he wanted to be with the cousins. When we actually did intend to take a family trip to see David and Molly and the cousins, we couldn't tell Sam until the last minute, because if we did he would camp at the front door days in advance, waiting to go, and all we would hear would be "Cousins, cousins, cousins."

Sam also made strange remarks from the time he was two and first able to talk. He would ask me why he couldn't live with his cousins. He would say, "If the cousins knew how much I wanted to go to their house, they would let me come over." He would also reproach me constantly: "Why can't you do that like Aunt Molly does it?" If I made a list of all the things he wanted me to do like Aunt Molly, it would be a mile long.

Once he asked, "Mom, when can I live with the cousins in the big house by the water with the big stairs?" I pointed out that the cousins live in a big house with big stairs now. He said, "Not that house, Mom. The other house. The stairs which didn't have carpet and I could hear them walking up and down the stairs. So when can I live in that house with them again?" I had no idea what he was talking about.

"You can't go live with the cousins, Sam. You live here."

Sam cried, insisting I let him go. He brought up the house by the water again a few days later. I cut him off with, "No, you can't go live with the cousins." He got angry and ran out of the room.

Sam was a high-energy child and he was often angry; he was so wound up inside he didn't know how to relax. But when we had these run-ins about the cousins or the way Aunt Molly does things, he would really lose it and throw an awful tantrum. I was completely baffled by his strange behavior. Looking back on it, I probably made it worse because he had worn me thin and I lost my patience with this cousins nonsense. I would tell him to stop talking about it, I didn't want to hear it, and no, we were not going to the cousins' house. I was always pushing back.

As he got older, Sam began insisting that Molly's family was his *real* family. I would have to explain to him that they weren't. This went on for about two years. About six months ago, when he was four, things began to escalate. These episodes usually happened in the car or while cuddling at bedtime, but this time it popped up while I was in the kitchen reading. Sam burst into the room mad, hands on hips, extremely excited, and asked, "Why isn't Kevin my big brother?"

I tried to stay cool. I explained to him that Kevin was his cousin, not his brother; Peyton was his brother. But Sam would not accept this. "Why isn't Kevin my big brother? Why are you keeping me here? I want to be with him right now. Why don't you ever listen to me, Mom?"

I said, "You have to stay here because this is where you live. We are your family. Peyton is your brother and Kevin is your cousin and nobody can change that."

He ran out of the kitchen, crying and whining between his sobs, "I want to be with *them*! Why does it have to be like this?"

## *"Why Didn't We Get Born, Mom?"*

Then one evening a few weeks later, we were all winding down before bedtime and Sam asked, "Mom, do you remember when I was in your tummy?"

I said, "Yes."

He asked, "Do you remember when Peyton was in your tummy?" Again I agreed. Then he said, "Do you remember when Peyton and I were in your tummy at the same time?"

I explained, "No, that's not the way it happened. You were in my tummy first, then you were born. Then Peyton was in my tummy, and then he was born." I pointed to Peyton, who was playing quietly on the floor, sucking on his pacifier.

Sam got a blank look on his face, like someone who has misplaced his car keys. Then he started laughing with relief and said, "Oh, now I remember. You're wrong, Mom! We were in Aunt Molly's tummy at the same time and we didn't get born!"

I felt like I had been punched in the stomach. I immediately understood what he was talking about. Sam and Peyton had been the twins that Molly lost ten years before my two children were born. Everything began to make sense. But before I could collect myself, Sam got very angry and began yelling at me, "Why didn't we get born, Mom? *Why didn't we get born?*"

Then, before I knew it, he took off after his little brother, screaming, "It's all your fault! I told you I wanted to get born really bad and you didn't want to! Tell me how you took me out of there!" I lunged at Sam and grabbed him and held him back because he was so furious I was afraid he would hurt his little brother. His anger really scared me. I told him to stop, that this was a crazy conversation, and he had no idea what he was talking about.

Sam stopped abruptly, spun around, and corrected me. He said he knew *exactly* what he was talking about. Again he confronted Peyton, yelling, "How did you do that?"

Peyton just sat there with his pacifier in his mouth, watching his brother. Peyton, unlike Sam, is a calm baby and rarely gets upset. But I was concerned how he would react to Sam's angry challenge. Peyton pulled the pacifier out of his mouth, and his little face got more angry than I have *ever* seen it. He yelled at his big brother, "I wanted *Daddy*!"

Sam fired back, "I didn't want Daddy, I wanted *Uncle David*!"

I was shocked. I yelled, "Sam!"

My scream shocked him back into his senses. Immediately he stopped trying to attack Peyton and his angry face turned very sad. "I'm sorry, Mom," he apologized. "I didn't mean it. I love Daddy, but I wanted Uncle David, too."

Not sure what to say, I offered, "Didn't anyone come here to be with *me*?"

That melted Sam. He came over and cuddled in my lap and said, "Mom, you're the best mom. I love you."

I started thinking about how I would explain this to my husband, Michael. Would he believe any of it? Then Sam said, "I've got to figure this out."

I said, "No, I've had enough of this conversation." We all started to calm down. Peyton went back to sucking on his pacifier.

But then Sam jumped up on the bed and started counting on his fingers. "First I was in Aunt Molly's tummy and I didn't get born. Then I tried to get back into Aunt Molly's tummy but Sophie [Molly's youngest daughter] was there in the way. So I tried to kick her out." Sam must have seen the surprised look on my face because he repeated, "I tried to kick her out and that didn't work, Mom! Then I got in your tummy and then I got born." He paused and then said in all seriousness, "I sure did work hard getting here, Mom!"

I didn't know what to say. He jumped off the bed and asked triumphantly, "Now can I go back and live with the cousins?"

This was all a little too much for me. I suggested we go get a drink of water. Sam took my hand as we walked down the steps. He asked me, "Does Peyton always have to follow me every time I'm born?" I told him I didn't know, that he probably remembered better than me.

He ran back up the steps to Peyton. I followed, curious to see how Peyton would react. Sam told his little brother what he had just remembered. Peyton started laughing. To my surprise he seemed to understand *completely*. I sat there thinking, "These two are talking about something that happened long before they were born, in a world completely unknown to me. And they're acting likes it's *normal*." It was all very strange.

## Switching Tummies

Although Sam is more vocal than his younger brother about all this, Peyton clearly has memories too. A few days after this outburst, I noticed that Peyton, who had just turned three, was staring at a picture of Uncle David hanging on the wall in our bedroom. I picked him up and said, "Do you want to see this picture?" He stared hard at it. I asked him, "Who is that, Peyton?"

He said, "Daddy." He repeated insistently, "Daddy. *Daddy!*"

About five pictures down from this was a picture of Michael, his father. I asked Peyton, "Well then, who is that?"

He had a very puzzled look on his face and questioned, "That's Daddy?" Then he pointed back to the picture of Uncle David and asked, "That's not Daddy?" I said, "No, that's not Daddy. It's Uncle David." A look of recognition dawned on his face and he muttered under his breath, "Oooh."

Recently we were making a homemade birthday card for Aunt Molly. I asked the kids what they wanted me to write on the card besides "Happy Birthday." Sam said to write, "I miss you and I want to see you soon." Peyton said, "Tell her I was her blue baby and now I'm Peyton and now I'm red."

I exclaimed, "What?" He repeated it in exactly the same words. I decided not to write that in the card. I wrote "I love you" instead as his contribution.

Sam and I reached a turning point one day in the car on the way to school. He told me about a dream he had. I wasn't sure if he really had the dream, or if he was gradually distancing himself from the direct memory. But he said it was a dream. He said, "I was two boys in Aunt Molly's tummy and then we had to switch tummies. Peyton was the other boy. Then he was really mad because he couldn't come with me *this* time and be in *your* tummy with me. He was *really* mad. You know what I mean, Mom?"

For the first time I didn't fight it. I confirmed to Sam, "Yes, I do. You were in Aunt Molly's tummy."

That was a big moment for me, because up until then I had resisted what he was trying to tell me and didn't want to hear any more about the cousins.

Then, in that moment, instead of pushing against him I joined him. And from that moment, Sam began to change. The arguments stopped.

I told Michael about these incidents. He didn't

know what to think, but he didn't laugh it off either. He thought it was time to tell Molly and David what was happening. The next time we visited them we broached the subject delicately, telling the story of some of the things Sam and Peyton had said. I was afraid how they would react.

But to my surprise Molly was *overjoyed*. She said it explained so many things: why she just *had* to be at the boys' births and why she loved them so much, like they were her own sons. She thanked us and told us what a great relief it was to know that her twins were back.

Getting it all out in the open gave us a chance to confirm some of the things that Sam had said. We asked her about the house near the water with uncarpeted stairs. She said, "Oh, my God. When I was pregnant with the twins, we lived in a house right on the bay; it was the only house we ever lived in that had uncarpeted stairs. We moved from that house three days before the twins died!"

Molly and I arranged for her to spend some time the next day alone with Sam. While they were together, she showed Sam a picture of herself pregnant with the twins. She asked him, "Do you know who's there in my tummy?"

Without hesitation he answered, "Me and Peyton."

She continued, "But you weren't born, Sam. Can you tell me *why* you weren't born?"

Sam thought about it for a second, and then told her about his dream where he was two boys and switched tummies. Molly, hoping for insight into the loss of her twins, asked again *why* he didn't come. But Sam just got a funny look on his face and wouldn't say anything more.

The next morning I asked him if he had told Aunt

Molly about the dream. He said that he really couldn't tell her everything. When I asked him why not, his response surprised me: "I couldn't tell her because *they* would laugh at me." I assured him that no one would laugh at him. He countered, "They would laugh at me because they know it's not allowed."

I didn't understand what he was saying and asked for clarification. "What's not allowed?"

He said, "Switching tummies. *I had to get permission for that.*" Then he got very quiet and guarded, as if someone were looking over his shoulder. I realized there was something that he wasn't supposed to tell and I wasn't supposed to know. So I dropped it.

Sam brightened and said, "Mom, I'm going to let you be my mom, and you can tell me what to do. Okay?" He said it like it was a solution that had just occurred to him.

I said, "Thank you, Sam. That will make my job a whole lot easier."

Since the day I acknowledged Sam's memories and he accepted me as his mother, his behavior has been totally different. He's not dark and angry anymore. He wakes up in the morning with a sunny smile on his face. He's much more relaxed and easygoing and his frequent temper tantrums have almost completely stopped. And he openly accepts us as his parents. Recently he told me, "I'm so glad I have you as my mom," and he told Michael, "I'm so glad I have you as my dad." We all feel much more at peace. (Sometimes, though, I still have to remind him that he gave me permission to be his mother.)

And Aunt Molly's life is changed too. She feels that if my two kids are the same souls as the twins she lost, she is blessed to have the privilege to be a part of their lives now. Last month she baby-sat Sam and Peyton on the anniversary of the twins' death. That was an emotional day for her. I know it helped her get closure on their deaths and get closer to Sam and Peyton.

## Facing Abortion

From the evidence in the previous cases of miscarriage and stillbirth, we see that the incoming soul can change its plans for the next lifetime and leave the womb at any point before birth. It can come back later to the same womb or go to a different mother. But what happens to the soul when it's the *mother* who chooses to terminate the pregnancy and has an abortion?

Abortion is a highly charged and polarizing issue in our culture. Abortion opponents—the pro-life side— equate terminating a pregnancy with murder and argue passionately for the protection of the unborn child's life. Inherent in this argument is the belief that the soul and physical body are inextricably joined from the moment of conception; so when the physical body is destroyed, the one chance that soul had for life on Earth is lost forever. Abortion proponents—the pro-choice side—argue just as passionately that a woman should have control over her own body and reproductive process, and should have the right to determine how many children she brings into the world. Inherent in this argument is the assumption that the fetus does not have the same rights as a person until it is born, or at least "viable." Layered on top of these personal views are secondary issues of social policy, religious doctrine, constitutional rights, and factional politics that make it even harder for a woman to sort out what to do when facing the heart-wrenching dilemma of an unwanted pregnancy.

I feel there is merit and good intention on both sides of the argument, with sincere, well-meaning people arguing for what they believe. At the same time, I believe there is another way to look at abortion, one that is seldom considered—from the perspective of the eternal soul traveling the reincarnation cycle.

The soul is indestructible. Soul consciousness does not die with the death of the physical body. It continues on after death, existing independently until it reincarnates. So, if the physical body is destroyed in an abortion, it won't terminate the soul's journey—though it may be a rather rude forced detour. The rerouted soul will change its plans and readjust the timing and circumstances of its rebirth. It could give up on the aborting mother and go to an entirely different family. Or, as cases show, if the pull to the first family of choice is strong, it will either wait for a more opportune time to enter the womb of the same mother or enter through another mother in the extended family. Some souls are incredibly persistent.

At the crux of the abortion issue, as I see it, are two questions. The first is: When does the soul merge with the forming physical body? And the second question: If the fetal body is destroyed, how does it affect the soul?

In the past these were exclusively metaphysical questions, impossible to answer with any finality. But the following cases and research offer new information that brings us closer than ever before to finding real answers. The picture that emerges gives us a new way of thinking about abortion. This new perspective, I believe, has something to offer both sides of the public debate and suggests an alternative view, possibly a middle ground between the two sides. But on the most personal level—to a mother facing the decision now, or living with the guilt of an abortion in the past—these findings offer a new and more discriminating, even spiritual, way of thinking about the petitioning soul. It suggests that abortion can be more a dialogue and negotiation, a delicate balance of spiritual concerns, between the soul and the mother.

## In and Out of the Forming Body

*When does the soul merge with the forming physical body?* When, exactly, does it plunge from heaven and commit to be born? This question, a perennial vexation to theologians and philosophers, intrigued Dr. Helen Wambach. She wondered: Does the soul consciousness merge with the body at conception or the first division of cells? Does it enter around the time the mother feels the first kick in the womb? Or at the moment of birth? To find the answer, she designed a study in which she took 750 hypnotic subjects through their prebirth experiences and then asked a number of questions, including "When does your soul enter the fetus?"

In analyzing their responses, in *Life Before Life*, Dr. Wambach found that "the subjects were unanimous on one key point: They felt *the fetus was not truly a part of their consciousness.* For most of the pregnancy they did not identify with the forming body. Rather, they existed fully conscious as an entity apart from the fetus. They frequently reported that the fetal body was confining and restrictive, and that they preferred the freedom of out-of-body existence. It was with much reluctance that many of them joined their consciousness with the cellular consciousness of the newborn infant."[1]

Only 11 percent of the subjects said they were aware of being inside the fetus at any time from conception to six months. This is surprising, since the first kick is usually felt around the fourth month. But the separate studies of Dr. Newton agree with Wambach.[2] He states that he has "*never* had a single case where a soul joined the fetus in the first trimester." It makes sense, though, in light of medical statistics that show that a fertilized egg has *less* than a 27 percent chance of surviving the first six weeks, and then only a 90 percent chance after that.[3] Would souls routinely become attached to a developing fetus that has such a slim chance of survival only to be turned away? Or does the soul enter later, when it is more likely that the fetus will survive?

A majority—89 percent—of Wambach's subjects responded that they didn't become involved with the fetus until after six months of gestation. Many reported that even then they weren't fully merged with the fetal body, but rather they moved in and out of it freely. One woman recalled that she entered the fetus only at the last minute, because she was "too happy and busy elsewhere" and was not interested in spending precious out-of-body time in confinement.[4]

The statistic I find most interesting in the context of the abortion question is that 33 percent reported they didn't join the fetus until the *last minute*, just before or during the birth process.

However, these late arrivals, as well as all other participants in this experiment, did recall hovering around their mothers, tuning in telepathically to her feelings during the pregnancy and watching what she did. Even if these souls didn't merge fully with the fetus until the last minute, they were aware of, and in touch with, the developing fetus, the mother, and even the family. It's like they were still in orbit, preparing to land.

There is ample evidence for this ability of the soul to remain independent and mobile throughout the pregnancy yet aware of everything happening in and around the mother. The soul consciousness seems to be able to perceive not only telepathically, but also as an observer watching from "above." I have quite a few cases in which children know details of specific events that happened before they were born. They were trailing their prospective parents and checking them out.

For example, one two-year-old boy recalled his mother severely cutting her finger and going to the hospital and having multiple stitches. He explained to his mother how he had been hovering above her watching the whole thing. What really pinned it down for her, though, was one detail the child remembered: He said she was wearing a yellow dress when she had the accident, and since it had gotten all bloody, she had thrown it away. This was entirely correct, but a detail the mother had completely forgotten until her son reminded her.

Dr. Wambach's conclusion that the soul can enter the fetus at any time during pregnancy is supported by a striking and puzzling pattern in Dr. Stevenson's work. He lists twenty-one cases in *Reincarnation and Biology* in which a child was born *less than nine months* after the previous personality died.[5] In other words, the new body was conceived and developing before the previous incarnation ended and the soul was liberated from the former body. Dr. Stevenson's evidence challenges the notion that the soul must enter the womb or be bound to the fetus at conception—or, at least, it challenges our need to view matters of the soul in strict linear time. This new revelation allows for some of the family return cases I've seen where there is less than nine months between death and rebirth.

## Negotiating Abortion

Are souls affected by an abortion? Do they carry feelings of fear, sadness, anger, or rejection as a consequence of being evicted from the womb? It's difficult to generalize about all aborted babies from a handful of cases of children who happen to remember the event. But like anything else involving the individual, different souls seem to respond to the event in different ways. Some children who remember being aborted are shaken and still haunted by the emotional shock. Others seem to take it in stride and are not affected at all.

I received the following e-mail from a mother who was convinced that her aborted child returned to her. He was still disturbed by the memory.

> When I became pregnant at forty-one, my doctors urged me to have an abortion because of my age and because I have a blood condition. They were afraid if I went through with the pregnancy, it would endanger my life.
>
> I was devastated by my predicament, and cried and begged for God's forgiveness because I believed that abortion is murder. But I had no choice and had to go through with the abortion, because I had a young son at home and could not risk dying and leaving him motherless.
>
> A year after I had the abortion, I became pregnant

again *despite* using birth control and being very cautious. This time I decided to go through with the pregnancy, no matter what the risk. I had a C-section and gave birth to a healthy baby boy we named Reese.

One day when Reese was three, we were driving somewhere on an errand when suddenly he began shaking and crying in his car seat. I was so surprised by this outburst, I pulled off the road into a parking lot and stopped the car. I couldn't see anything that could have caused him to get so upset. I asked, "What's wrong, Reese?"

He stuttered through his tears: "When I was in your belly before, a snake came and ate me up. Then I went to a land of rainbows. An angel came and asked me what I wanted to do. I told the angel I wanted to come back to you, Mommy."

I cried as Reese told his story, because I remembered that the doctor who performed the abortion had used some kind of surgical tool that looked like a snake—just as Reese had described it. Until that moment, I had never believed in reincarnation. But I have no doubt that Reese really remembered being the child I aborted, and now I believe reincarnation is real.

I saw that Reese was troubled by strong emotional memories from being aborted. But after he talked about it, his feelings seemed to resolve, and after that day he never mentioned the abortion again.

From that experience with my son, I feel compelled to tell people my story to warn them that the soul of an unborn child *does* have feelings and can be affected by abortion. At the same time, I want mothers to be comforted to know that their aborted baby *can* return to them as another child.

And I thank God for giving my little boy back to me.

If some souls are upset when they are aborted and others brush it off, perhaps these different reactions have something to do with the degree to which the soul identified with the forming fetus. If the incoming soul hasn't completely joined the fetus at the time of the abortion, it may experience the event from the point of view of an observer, emotionally unattached. But if the soul joined with the fetus early, the abortion may feel more like a personal violation and cause emotional stress, as in Reese's case.

Past life researchers suggest that some souls are aware during the life-planning process that there's a good chance they will be aborted. Although the action is always an assertion of the mother's free will, there may have been a karmic agreement between the incoming soul and the mother, made even before *she* was born, to participate in the event for the mutual benefit of their interweaving souls. From our perspective, it's difficult to fathom why a soul would choose to enter a womb, only to be thwarted in its attempts to be born. But from the perspective of many lifetimes, the experience might be the vehicle for a soul to learn particular, necessary lessons that can be learned only through taking a body, even for a very short time.

The next case, from Gladys McGarey, M.D., is one of those in which a child remembered being aborted but was not upset about it. She tells the story in her pioneering book *Born to Live*.

A mother took her four-year-old out for lunch. Quite out of the blue the child remarked, "The last time I was a little girl, I had a different mommy!" The girl continued, "But that wasn't the last time. Last time, when I was four inches long and in your tummy, Daddy wasn't ready to marry you yet, so I went away. But then I came back." Her eyes lost that faraway look and again she was chatting about four-year-old matters.

The mother was stunned silent. No one but her husband and her doctor knew this. She had indeed become pregnant two years before she and her husband were ready to get married. She was ready to have the child, but her husband-to-be was not. At four months she had an abortion.

When the two of them did get married and were ready to have their first child, the same entity made its appearance. And the little child was saying, in effect, "I don't have any resentments toward you for having had the abortion. I understood. I knew why it was done, and that's okay. So here I am again . . . let's get on with the business of life."[6]

Although this child seemed to be unaffected by the memory, Dr. McGarey was deeply changed by the mother's story. She had been practicing obstetrics for more than thirty years, but she had no idea that an aborted baby could return to the same mother as a later child—and remember it. She quickly saw the implications for counseling other mothers with unwanted pregnancies. This was a new and vastly different way of looking at abortion because it embraced the perspective of the conscious incoming soul. She reasoned: If the soul who wishes to be born is aware, conscious of what is happening with the mother before birth, why not try to *include* it in the decision whether or not to abort?

Intrigued by the possibility, she promptly put the idea to a practical test. A pregnant fifteen-year-old came to her office for abortion counseling. Dr. McGarey advised the girl and her family to pray about it, listen for guidance, and ask for dreams before making a decision. She prepared them to be open for any communication from the incoming soul. After following Dr. McGarey's suggestions, the girl and her family reached the same conclusion—they had to go through with the abortion. Dr. McGarey began to make arrangements for the procedure. But the next morning the family called saying the girl had aborted spontaneously. Dr. McGarey wondered why this happened. Did the baby's soul get the message and leave on its own?

From that point on, Dr. McGarey continued to experiment with this expanded form of communication between mother and incoming soul. She routinely encouraged her patients to communicate with their unborn child before making any firm decision about ending a pregnancy. She suggested they dialogue by writing down the reasons they felt they couldn't go through with the pregnancy and "listening" for the baby's response. After dialoguing in this way, some women decided to keep the baby, some decided to abort. But *some* of those who decided to abort had *spontaneous* abortions—they miscarried—before they could keep their appointment for the medical procedure. After seeing a number of these spontaneous abortions, Dr. McGarey concluded that the first case with the fifteen-year-old girl was not an anomaly.

She explains in her book how the experiences of the women she worked with convinced her that if the circumstances really aren't good for continuing the pregnancy and bringing that baby into the world at that time, the soul is willing to go away and wait for a better time, "in much the same way that a host may say to a guest who proposes a visit that it isn't the right time, but six months later everything will be all right. The person can then agree to come back in six months, or perhaps give up the idea of the visit. As conscious beings, if we communicate with the baby and explain the circumstances, then the baby can choose. In this way, the process of abortion becomes a spiritual act, one coming from love and concern, not just a mechanical, medical procedure."[7]

For more than twenty years now, other physicians and therapists have followed Dr. McGarey's lead when counseling women with unwanted pregnancies. Like Dr. McGarey, they facilitate dialogues between the mother and the spirit of the unborn child. They confirm her original discovery that dialoguing in this way allows the mother to express her sadness, guilt, anger, and all the other complex emotions that accompany an unwanted pregnancy in a nonjudgmental setting. And it enables the mother to communicate clearly and directly to the spirit of the child all the reasons she can't go through with the pregnancy. If the child's soul is truly receptive to communication from the mother, and the mother decides to abort, the soul will not be turned away feeling confused and hurt. Instead, it will understand why it is not being allowed to enter this particular mother at this particular time.[8]

## Don't Worry Mommy, That Was Me

Too often, though, mothers are not aware that this communication is possible, and they have absolutely no idea the baby they aborted can return to them. So, many years after an abortion, a mother can still suffer deeply from sadness, remorse, and guilt for her actions. Yet, as the following story shows, it's never too late for a mother to apologize to a soul and explain what happened—even if the dialogue is with a soul who has returned to her as another child.

A mother from Texas describes what happened:

My child is now twenty-four years old, but I have never forgotten what he said long ago when he was just three.

One day, Joel and I were driving home from his preschool. He was sitting next to me coloring while I listened to an abortion debate on the radio. Suddenly he piped up, "Abortion is wrong," and I about fell over. I didn't realize he was even listening or knew what the word *abortion* meant.

Not wanting my young son to learn to judge others so quickly, I explained, "Joel, abortion is a woman's choice. When I was sixteen I made a mistake and had to have an abortion. I always felt sad about that, but I did what I felt I had to do at the time."

I always carried much guilt about my abortion, and talking to my son about it brought up all the emotion and sadness that I had tried to push away. I couldn't tell if he understood or heard what I said, because he kept on coloring.

Then Joel said, in such a matter-of-fact way he could have been talking about something he did in preschool, "Don't worry, Mommy. That was me. I just went back to heaven and waited for you." He never even lifted his head up from his coloring book.

From that day on, I've had a peace in my life that I hadn't known since I was sixteen.

# Chapter 8

## Announcing Dreams

*In the dream, his face glowed from within. As he smiled so beautifully and peacefully, he said, "I know you—I already know you. We'll be together soon." And then with one last comforting smile, he was gone. I get tears remembering this dream because it was such a special gift. He made me feel like we had known each other for eternity.*

Souls are busy in the afterlife. Not only do they plan and negotiate their next incarnation, but in some cases they *communicate* with mortals on Earth. They send messages to loved ones left behind to assure them they are "alive" and well in the spirit world. And then, before some souls reincarnate, they communicate to the chosen family: "I'm coming! Prepare for me!" If a soul has chosen to return to the same family it left behind, this may be the first sign that a deceased relative is planning to return.

While these otherworldly communications can

occur at any time during the soul's journey along the continuum of consciousness, they tend to be most frequent soon after death and just before conception and birth. The modes of both after-death and prebirth communication are similar—they are actually two sides of the same thing. Souls can make themselves known to us through waking visions, sounds and voices, even smells and touch. But by far the most common channel for both after-death and prebirth communication is dreams. *Announcing dreams,* as they are called, are especially prevalent in prebirth communication, and are a common feature of same-family cases.

Prebirth and after-death communication can be compared to radio messages received from a ship sailing at sea. As the ship sails away it maintains contact with the port until it reaches the limit of the radio signals; then the messages get fuzzy and finally stop altogether. As the ship again approaches shore, the messages resume and are more audible. In the same way, a recently departed soul sends messages of love and concern to relatives back on Earth, but after a while the communication becomes less frequent. Perhaps this is because the soul's need to contact loved ones on Earth diminishes as it progresses through the spirit world and lets go of attachments and concerns from the last life. But as the soul prepares to return to a new body, it resumes sending messages—either to a new family on a distant shore, or to the family it left behind at port. In exceptional cases, the soul never ventures far from shore and stays in touch with the family during the full interim between death and rebirth.

Prebirth communication is an important part of same-family reincarnation. True, it can occur before the arrival of an unfamiliar soul as well. But it is most meaningful—and most dramatic—in cases of same-family reincarnation because the family is able to recognize the signs associated with that particular soul.

If you accept the possibility of communication from a soul on the other side and learn the different forms it can take, you will be prepared to recognize the signs when they come. You will open yourself to receive messages lovingly sent to you from the spirit world—especially those heralding a joyous reunion with a person you loved before death took them away.

## Leaving Port

A surprising number of people have had direct communication from deceased loved ones, and in the last couple of decades they have begun to talk openly about it. For this reason, after-death communication is now better known and better documented than prebirth communication. Since the modes of communication are essentially the same for both, we can look first at the more familiar forms of after-death communication to know what to look for when souls similarly communicate their imminent return.

It is not uncommon for surviving relatives to see their deceased loved ones, hear their voices, or feel their presence. This communication is sporadic, sometimes vague, and usually subtle. Because most people don't know that communication between this world and the world of spirit is even possible, these opportunities are often missed or written off as coincidence, just an eerie feeling, or an overly active imagination—when, in fact, a deceased relative is trying to make contact.

The spirits communicate by appealing directly to any of our senses. Sometimes they can be seen. A spirit, or disembodied soul, appears as an apparition— a fluid, energetic form of a person. I experienced this myself at the first family gathering after my father's death. I caught a glimpse of his translucent form gliding through the long entrance hallway of my house. It was quick. But it made a lasting impression on me.

According to authors Bill and Judy Guggenheim, who document many forms of after-death communication in *Hello from Heaven*, a soul can also make its presence known through the sense of smell. A scent or fragrance we closely associate with the deceased—the smell of roses, pipe tobacco, or a favorite cologne or cream, for example—suddenly materializes when there is no possible source for the smell. Any smell bypasses the logical thought process, so we know instantly, before thinking, that the deceased is present. The unique association of the smell is the deceased's way of saying, "Yes, I'm here with you."

Hearing is another channel the deceased can use to communicate. The survivor may hear the deceased speaking as a voice "outside the head" or hear messages telepathically in the mind. This can be the result of a dialogue initiated by the survivor through prayer or petitioning. Or it can happen spontaneously, as words or phrases instantly enter the mind.

Any of these sensory experiences can be accompanied by palpable feelings in the body: chills, waves of warmth, or surges of energy that run through the body. Sometimes, a spirit will make itself known through a comforting touch on the cheek, a pat on the shoulder, or a full-bodied hug.

## Pink Toy Telephone

It shouldn't come as a surprise that young children are more receptive to after-death communication than adults. I suspect this is true because they have recently returned from the spirit world. They haven't been trained or conditioned yet *not* to believe what they are perceiving, so it is not unusual for them to see grandparents, a parent, or a sibling who has passed on and have a full conversation with them. These conversations are not the usual one-sided monologues we associate with imaginative play; they are full two-way dialogues with appropriate pauses as the child listens. Sometimes, the child will relay specific messages that shock the adults, because they contain accurate information or details about the deceased the child could not have known.

I have an extraordinary case of past life memory that begins not with the reincarnated child, but with a little sister, Lauren, who dialogued with her brother after he died. Nadine, the mother, describes what she saw:

A few months after my sixteen-year-old stepson, Roger, died in a car accident, two-year-old Lauren began talking to him on her pink toy telephone. These frequent conversations were long, animated, and filled with laughter. They were uncanny because little Lauren would pause at all the appropriate points in the conversation. Even older kids playing telephone don't know to pause.

I would ask, "Who are you talking to today?"

She would always answer, "Roger. Roger called me on my telephone."

This happened so often over a year's time, we

didn't think much of it. Then, one day as Lauren was sitting in her high chair happily making a mess of her spaghetti dinner, she announced to me, "You know, Roger said he's coming back very soon."

I didn't want to burst her bubble, but I felt I had to be honest with her. I explained, "No, honey, Roger is not coming back because he died. He's in heaven now."

Lauren insisted, "But I've been talking to him and he told me he's coming back!" Then she added importantly, "And he's coming back a lot sooner than you think."

I let her remark go, thinking she was too young to understand what death is.

A few days later we were shopping at the Belk Store at the mall and Lauren pulled me to a display of clothes for infant boys. I thought she wanted me to buy her some clothes and tried to steer her away, explaining that these were for little boys, not little girls.

But Lauren said, "We have to get some for Roger. He's coming back." Again I was surprised by her insistence. She was certain Roger was coming back and she wanted me to get ready.

I filed these incidents away and didn't think about them much until a few years later after Donald was born and started saying all those amazing things.

Nadine's son Donald was born a year later after what the doctors called an "impossible pregnancy" for the forty-three-year-old mother. As he grew up he made dozens of accurate and startling remarks about the auto accident, changes in the house since Roger's death, and events that happened when Roger was still alive, which proved to everyone familiar with the case that Donald was Roger reborn.

In retrospect, Nadine is convinced that Lauren's conversations with her deceased brother on the pink toy telephone were real and that he really had informed her of his imminent return. Nadine sent me a marvelously prescient snapshot taken the Christmas before Roger died. In the photo, a dark-haired teenage boy is beaming down at his baby sister, who is holding the pink telephone to her ear—the same pink phone the two later used to communicate after he died.

## I'll See You in My Dreams

Although spirits employ a wide variety of means for communicating with the living, dreams are the most common form of direct communication. Dreams are a meeting ground between the worlds. Researchers Joel Martin and Patricia Romanowski report in their book, *Love Beyond Life,* that the most profound and long-lasting communications occur in this state. They suggest the reason is that during the dream state it might be easier for the spirit to make contact with the living because, while asleep, our rational filters are down and our minds are most flexible and receptive to nonordinary experiences. Another intriguing possibility is that during sleep *we* leave our bodies and astral-travel, meeting the deceased in a dimension accessible to both of us, a neutral territory for disembodied travelers.

Whatever the mechanism, these dreams—which are more aptly described as *visitations*—are highly significant for the dreamer. They are far more real and vivid than ordinary dreams. In them, dreamers clearly see and embrace deceased loved ones who appear as they did in life, or if they were sick before they died, they appear in full health. When dreamers awaken from one of these vivid encounters, they feel as if they actually visited with the deceased. These impressions, unlike ordinary dreams, are fixed in the memory and stay with the dreamer for a long time, even years after the experience.

Because dreams tend to last longer than other communications from the deceased, they provide an opportunity for prolonged and meaningful messages. Communication within these visitations is usually telepathic, without spoken words, traveling directly from one mind to the other. Even when messages are symbolic, they rarely require analysis, unlike ordinary dreams. Their meaning is close to literal and easily understood. Sometimes they are solely messages of comfort and reassurance; some accurately foretell future events or give the dreamer solutions to problems or answers to questions.

After-death communication is most common in the days and weeks following death and for several years thereafter. Then direct communication may stop—but not always. There are no absolute rules. After many years of silence, the deceased may resume contact for no apparent reason, or in times of difficulty or danger. The deceased may appear in a moment of crisis and communicate a warning, helpful instructions, or assurance that all will be well.

## Returning to Port

Most people have never heard of prebirth communication or announcing dreams. Until recently, no one attempted to document or research the phenomenon.

And because it is such a personal experience, it is almost impossible for an outsider to verify. It is seldom discussed in public; the mothers and fathers who have experienced it know it's true for them, but they keep it to themselves, or at best, share their experiences as curious stories over coffee or in play groups.

Prebirth communication is similar to the soul's communication after death in its subtlety and use of any of the five senses as a channel. But its purpose is different. The incoming spirit is signaling its intention to be born into a particular family.

Prebirth communication can occur prior to conception, anytime during the pregnancy, or immediately before or after birth. The souls reveal themselves to a mother-to-be or other family member in announcing dreams, visions, or by "speaking." In one way or another, they announce, "I'm coming!" But the dreams, visions, or messages can also give specific information that helps the parents understand who is coming to them to be their child.

Like after-death communication, prebirth communication is nothing new. In many non-Western cultures, preexistence is taken for granted, and prebirth communication is expected. Tibetan Buddhists employ dreams to help them locate the next incarnation of their spiritual leaders. In our Judeo-Christian culture, stories and legends of spirit messages announcing a celebrated birth stretch back to the earliest days of our history. The best-known references can be found in the Bible. In the Gospel of Luke, for example, the angel Gabriel reveals to Zacharias that his wife, Elizabeth, will have a son in her old age (an "impossible pregnancy") and that he should be named John. Gabriel then visits the Virgin Mary in Galilee and—well, you know the rest of the story. But since we have developed a "modern," rational worldview that denigrates any phenomenon that can't be reproduced in the laboratory, these types of communications have been written off as overactive imagination, wishful thinking, "old wives' tales," or superstition.

Times are changing, though, for prebirth communication. Two women researchers, among others, are seriously studying these stories. Each had prebirth communications with their own children, and because the messages were so compelling and real, they began seeking out other parents who had these experiences too. Elisabeth Hallett, author of *Soul Trek: Meeting Our Children on the Way to Birth*, and Sarah Hinze, author of *Coming from the Light*, working independently and unaware of each other's research, collected hundreds of examples of prebirth communication. They both documented visual, auditory, and telepathic communications, which often foretell a pregnancy, reveal the sex of the child, and may even give a peek at the appearance and personality of the child.

According to both Hallett and Hinze, it is not uncommon for a prospective mother to sense a baby's spirit hovering about her before conception. I experienced this, too, before my pregnancies. Women report feeling they're being trailed by the loving presence of a baby's spirit seeking to enter their womb. Interestingly, the concept of a spirit trailing a mother is consistent with reports from young children who say they remember hovering around the mother.

As in after-death communications, spirits sometimes appear as childlike forms in fleeting waking visions. It is difficult to know how many of these visions are real or are just the projections of a parent's imagination. But according to the researchers, there are enough cases in which the visions proved to be so accurate, matching the appearance of the child after it was born, that the parents were convinced they actually had been given a prebirth glimpse of their child.

## Announcing Dreams

Again, as with after-death communication, the most common communication from the future child comes in dreams. Of course, dreams of anticipation, stimulated by excitement and maternal hormones, are a natural part of pregnancy. But some dreams are so vivid, so coherent, that they stand out from the rest. In these, the dreamer, who is usually the mother-to-be, has the distinct and unforgettable sensation of actually meeting the future child in the dream state.

Announcing dreams occur in all cultures in all parts of the world. They appear so regularly in Dr. Stevenson's cases, he considers them a standard feature of a "fully developed" rebirth case, along with statements, behaviors, and birthmarks. Although he doesn't count dreams as evidence because they are too ephemeral to prove, he does take the time to record and cross-check what the mother said about the dream before the baby was born. Then, if the child's past life memory is verified using statements, behaviors, and birthmarks, he goes back and credits the dream as the first clue to the former identity of the child. This is as close as we can come to proving the truth of announcing dreams. This, and the abundance of announcing dreams reported all over the world.

In an announcing dream, either a full-grown person or a baby appears to the dreamer and declares its intention to be her child. The disembodied spirit may communicate its intentions directly by saying, "I'm coming!" or "I want to stay with you" or "Prepare for me." Sometimes the spirit petitions for entry, asking, "May I be your child?" or something to that effect. The message may not always be so verbal and direct; it can be visual and symbolic. The person appearing in the dream may enter the dreamer's bedroom and climb into bed between the husband and wife, or the spirit may stand at the foot of the bed, or appear as a child who sits on the lap of the dreamer.

One mother from St. Louis told the following story to Elisabeth Hallett, which she posted on her Web site:

> About two years prior to my son's conception, I was in the exciting beginning of my new career as a psychotherapist. Enjoying my "calling," I decided to forgo having children.
>
> One night I had a very vivid dream. A toddler appeared to me and said, "Mommy, when are you going to be ready for me?"
>
> I replied, still in the dream, "Who are you?"
>
> He answered, "I am Timothy, your son."
>
> I awoke startled—startled and instantly different. Changed. I felt a beautiful sense of peace and love. After that, Timothy appeared in my dreams often until a year later when I conceived my first child. The pregnancy was not planned or expected.
>
> Of course I named my new son Timothy. Timothy is now a toddler and looks remarkably like the child who introduced himself to me in my dreams.[1]

In the majority of cases like these, the incoming spirit is someone unknown to the parent-to-be. In some, though, the incoming spirit is a deceased relative the dreamer recognizes. In the dream, a familiar image in a familiar voice declares something to the effect of "I'm coming back!"

The following case was reported to me in an e-mail from Ned, an attorney who lives near Washington, D.C.

My father, Jimmy, died in early 1997 after a long battle with Parkinson's disease. For more than a year our family stood vigil at my father's bedside, though he could barely recognize any of us.

Very soon after my father's death, my wife became pregnant. Around the time the baby was due, my wife dreamed of my father on three consecutive nights. In the first two dreams, my father appeared at the foot of her bed and gazed at her lovingly without saying a word. On the third night he appeared as before, but this time he said two words: "It's time." At that very moment the dream ceased and she woke up with a start and simultaneously felt the first contraction of labor.

Our daughter, Emily, was born the next day. Emily is now a toddler and she has shown so many unmistakable similarities to my father that we jokingly call her "Daddy." No one has to believe me, and no one has to agree with my conclusion, but I will not waver from my belief that my father has returned as my daughter.

## Phantom Fly-bys

I first heard this story when Cindy shared it with a large audience at a workshop I gave at the ARE (The

Edgar Cayce Foundation) in Virginia Beach. It is filled with examples of after-death and prebirth communication, including many dreams, that span the arc between her brother-in-law's death and rebirth into the family. In fact, it seems as if he stayed close by and was never completely out of touch with his family during his stay in heaven. I've taken the story from the tape of the workshop, Cindy's e-mails, and private conversations with her.

Grant Merrill died on August 5, 1987, in a small plane crash. He was my husband's brother, but I never knew him. He and his best friend were "trick-flying" in the mountains near Aspen, Colorado, when the plane went out of control and they crashed. Kevin (my future husband) was waiting at the Aspen airport when he got the tragic news. No one knows exactly what happened, but both men died instantly.

It was a devastating loss for the whole Merrill family. Grant was clever, well liked, and he was just hitting his stride in his career—he owned a successful engineering firm in California that he had founded after graduating from Stanford. Although I was acquainted with the family since I was a little girl—Kevin and I went to school together—I had never met Grant, and I didn't marry Kevin until a few years after Grant's death. But because the family missed him so much and kept his memory alive, I felt as if I knew him.

The family also believed Grant was keeping his own memory alive, staying in touch in curious ways the whole time between his death and the month I conceived Mason, exactly seven years later.

The first sign that we interpreted as communication

from Grant happened in Aspen when the family gathered at Grant's favorite ski run to dispose of his ashes. It was a perfect late-summer day with Colorado-blue skies. Just as they were throwing his ashes into the wind, everyone clearly heard the sound of a single-engine plane overhead. It sounded close by, but there wasn't a plane in sight. Yet everyone agreed they had heard it. No one could figure it out.

These phantom fly-bys happened often—whenever the Merrill family gathered outdoors for a special occasion. It got to the point that everyone began to expect one and listen for it. I first witnessed one at our wedding at the family farm in Kentucky. During the ceremony we clearly heard a single-engine plane—the sound was even captured on our wedding video. But, as before, when family members looked up to locate the plane in the sky, there was nothing in sight.

Grant's fiancée, Sheri, received the next "visitation." She had taken his death as hard as anyone. One day, shortly after the crash, she was having an exceptionally hard day. She was sitting alone in her room crying and talking to Grant, begging and praying for some sign that he could hear her. Suddenly a little figurine he had given her started to move. It was a porcelain figurine of two lovers sitting together on a swing. The swing started rocking gently back and forth on its own. Then it began spinning and swinging very fast. Sheri said there was no question it was moving on its own; everything else in the room was perfectly still. Needless to say, this completely blew her mind and she was convinced it was Grant telling her he was with her and could hear her.

His sister, Carol, felt his presence whenever she was riding her horse at the family farm. She knew he was watching her. Carol rode often to bring herself healing and comfort.

Grant's father, Jim, was a recently born-again Christian and had been grieving as much for the fact that Grant was not "saved" when he died as he was for Grant himself. Jim's newfound faith had been a sore spot between father and son—Grant thought his dad had gone overboard with the whole Christianity thing. That didn't stop Jim from praying and praying for some sort of sign from God that his son had gone on to heaven despite not being saved. Shortly after the crash he got a phone call from a business acquaintance. The man said Grant had come to him in a vivid dream with a message he felt compelled to deliver. The message was, "Tell my father that I am okay. Everything is all right with me. Don't worry." This message was a great comfort to Jim.

## Teaching Dreams

My husband, Kevin, was the biggest skeptic in the family. He dearly loved his brother, and missed him terribly. But he was a very rational "left-brain" person like his brother, and he couldn't believe that any of these signs were really messages from the dead. He kept saying to me, "There must be some explanation, we're just not seeing it." Still, he knew the signs comforted his family, so he publicly went along with it for the sake of the others.

In this spirit, Kevin joined his mother, Anne, on a visit to a well-known medium shortly after Grant's death in hopes that a message from him would help Anne's grieving process. Carol went along too.

The first message the medium delivered was to Carol: Grant wanted her to know he was indeed with her when she rode her horse at the farm. She received other messages and assurances that comforted Anne. Then she said Grant was very upset about his Jeep—that he had left things unfinished. Nobody knew what this meant. Her last message from Grant was directed to Kevin: Grant wanted his shoes back. That comment was as mysterious as the thing about the unfinished Jeep.

Soon after, when Kevin went to California to gather up Grant's belongings, he found his Jeep up on cinder blocks in his garage; Grant had been rebuilding the engine, but obviously hadn't been able to finish it. A month later Kevin was cleaning out his own closet and found a pair of Grant's shoes he had borrowed, but completely forgotten about, stuffed in a duffel bag. Kevin was shaken by the accuracy of these messages. But he still had difficulty believing they were from Grant. He said the medium got lucky, that's all.

About a year after Grant's death Kevin started having a series of vivid dreams about his brother. They continued, sporadically, until the summer of 1994, and then stopped abruptly—almost seven years to the day after Grant's death. Of all of these signs, I believe Kevin's dreams were the most significant because they broke through his skepticism. He started to change his ideas as a result of the dreams.

Kevin described the dreams as being very different from regular dreams. He called them "teaching dreams." He said he has no doubt he was actually talking to his brother. Of all the dreams he had, the last one stands out as the most memorable.

In this dream, Kevin is walking through a forest and

runs into Grant. He's shocked to see him and asks, "Why are you here? How can this be?" Grant says, "Don't worry about that. Relax and enjoy this moment we have together. Isn't it wonderful?"

Then Grant starts to teach. "Life is a continuum," he explains. "Life is like a circle with a line from one end to the other. Our life is moving across this line." Kevin gets the impression that death is at the other end of the line. But he doesn't really understand, and Grant explains again. Still Kevin doesn't get it, so Grant draws a diagram to help him visualize it. He draws a perfectly round circle and straight lines—it has the precision of an engineer's drawing.

Kevin understands from the drawing that a person's life is represented by traveling down one of the lines across the circle, and then you die. But you don't just die. You take off again and start over, coming down another line.

Grant continues, "The best part is reuniting with people when their lines cross again." Kevin understands Grant is talking about multiple lifetimes. Here the diagram clearly shows how different lines on the circle intersect over and over, representing the re-unions between people in different lifetimes. Then Grant starts naming people Kevin knows who are to-gether now in this life and who also knew each other in previous lives. "But," Grant adds, "they don't have a memory of this now." Then he looks directly at Kevin and says, "I'm getting ready to come back down one of those lines again. I'll see you."

Then Kevin woke up. He shook me awake and told me his dream. It was so vivid, he remembered it all. He was excited because the dream was so clear. Even the diagram was still fresh in his mind, so I suggested he draw it and write down everything, which he did.

## Endless and Familiar

The signs from Grant were most frequent right after he died. Except for Kevin's constant dreams, they gradually subsided for the rest of the family. Until, that is, the summer of 1994, around the time Kevin had his last dream.

Then I had my dream. It happened while I was taking a nap at the family farm. In my dream I was sitting on a rooftop watching various flying contraptions soaring and circling all around me. They were bizarre and unusual vehicles, not your typical airplanes or helicopters. Suddenly I recognized Grant in one of the contraptions flying by. I waved to him and begged him to come talk to me. "Grant, Grant, come here. I want to talk to you."

Suddenly he was perched beside me on the rooftop, and I said, "Hi, how are you? I've always wanted to know you. Please stay."

He said, "Gotta go!" and he started to take off.

I said, "No, no, please wait. I really want to get to know you."

He turned toward me and I will never forget the *radiant* smile he gave me. His face glowed from within and his eyes were endless and familiar. As he smiled so beautifully and peacefully, he said, "I know you— I already know you. We'll be together soon."

And then, with one last comforting smile, he was gone. I get tears remembering this dream because it was such a special gift. He made me feel like we had known each other for eternity.

Shortly after that dream, in the early fall of 1994, I conceived Mason, and all the dreams and communications from Grant stopped abruptly for me and everyone else in the family.

## *Mason*

Mason was born in May 1995. For the first few years of his life, there were many things he said and did that convinced me he is the reincarnation of Grant. Almost all involve airplanes.

My first indication that something was going on came when Mason was only one month old. One day, I was breast-feeding him out on the back deck when a small plane flew overhead. At the first sound of the plane, Mason, who was always an eager eater and never stopped nursing for *anything*, abruptly stopped, twisted around to see the plane, and gazed up into the sky for the longest time. He waited and listened until the plane was no longer in range before going back to nursing. I remember getting chills down my spine because that was the first time he had ever heard a plane, in this lifetime at least, and he was totally mesmerized by it.

When Mason was nine months old he began having nightmares. Each time, he woke up shaking and sobbing. These were different from the typical "waking up at night" episodes caused by normal discomfort. When he had these nightmares, he wouldn't look at me and didn't seem to know who I was. It was impossible to console him when he was in that state. I would have to wait until he finally exhausted himself from crying and fell asleep. These nightmares occurred about twice a month until he was more than two years old.

When Mason was two and finally old enough to verbalize his feelings, I would try to ask him what was wrong when he woke up sobbing. Finally, one night, I got through to him. When I asked him what was wrong, he wailed out very distinctly, "My airplane is crashing! My airplane is crashing!" Those were his exact words. I immediately began to shake and cry when he said this. And I thought to myself, "I wish Kevin were here! He'll never believe me when I tell him!" After that the nightmares were less frequent, and finally they stopped.

Mason has talked about his airplane crashing many times since that night. Once, when we were riding in the car, we passed a serious car accident. Without thinking I said, "Oh, my God. Oh, my God! I hope no one died." As I said it, I thought I might have scared Mason, but then I thought, "Well, he won't know what *died* means anyway."

But Mason, who had been sitting very quietly in his car seat said, "Oh, Mommy, *died,* you mean like when your airplane crashes and you die?" I couldn't believe my ears! At that point we had never discussed death, dying, or plane crashes with two-year-old Mason. His remark flustered me so, I almost had an accident myself. It was definitely one of those "hair standing on end" moments.

Mason is utterly fascinated with airplanes of any size or kind, with how they fly, and how they crash. He has every possible airplane toy. His preschool teachers assume that Mason's father flies planes for a living because he talks about planes so much at school. Kevin has a remote-control plane, and Mason can't get enough of it.

At his third birthday party, we had a piñata airplane filled with candy. That was a mistake! Everything at the party was going fine until it was time to break open the piñata. Mason began crying hysterically when the other children started hitting it with the stick. He cried, "They're hurting it! Make them stop!" It took a very long time to quiet him down.

One day, when he was three, we were watching TV and channel surfing when we came across a program about plane crashes—of all things. I quickly changed the channel because I didn't want him to see it. But it was too late. Mason got agitated and cried, "Mommy, turn it back! Were those planes crashing? I want to see them!" When I refused, he became extremely angry with me, which is really out of character for him. I had to give in and let him watch. After the show he quizzed me for over a half hour asking why each plane crashed. He needed to go over it again and again until he understood exactly what had happened with each plane.

We fly on the airlines a lot to visit my parents, and Mason loves flying. But every time he gets on a plane with me he asks, very casually, "Mommy, are we going to crash?"

I say, "No, sweetie, we're not going to crash."

He says, "Okay," and then he's fine.

Now Mason is five and most of these signs have stopped. Early on, when the nightmares and the eerie coincidences were frequent, it all seemed more real to me. Back then I was convinced that Mason was Grant reincarnated. Now, I still believe it in my heart, but because he's older and the signs aren't as prevalent, it's harder to feel it so deeply. I guess that's normal with the passage of time. If Grant has returned, my wish is that he can accomplish, through Mason, all the things he left unfinished when he died in that plane crash. I hope he can fulfill the dreams and desires that drew him, so strongly and quickly, back to this planet Earth.

## Annunciation

When parents are blessed with a prebirth communication from an incoming spirit, it can do more than just introduce the new soul to the family. The dreams or visions may give specific information to the parents about the child's identity, past life history, and advice on how to care for the child's special needs after it is born. The messages help the family prepare.

The following story came to me in a single e-mail and because it is so beautifully written, I've included it here in full. Although it is not a case of same-family reincarnation, it is a dramatic illustration of a prebirth vision giving specific, detailed instructions to parents to help them with their child's special emotional needs. It is interesting to note, too, that this message did not come directly from the child, but from an angel or spirit guide who was watching over the boy's birth. I suspect it was one of those guides or angels who help souls plan their lives before they return to Earth.

I am a forty-five-year-old CPA currently working as tax director for a large corporation in Denver. My son, Mark, was born in 1988. I was present in the hospital delivery room when he was born. Immediately before his birth a very powerful force surrounded me, and I felt it was giving me a message. The message was not in sequential sentences like a person speaking, but a sort of "quantum" packet of information my brain understood in full immediately without having to translate it into a sequential thinking pattern. (This is difficult to explain, but I think you may understand.) My initial thought was that this was an angel communicating a message to me. I did not actually see any angelic beings, but I could definitely sense a presence which I felt to be almost directly above me, slightly toward my left. My eyes instinctively looked up in that direction as these feelings came over me. This all happened in about two or three seconds.

The message I sensed was this: "This precious child is one of the marines killed in the barracks explosion in Beirut in 1983. You must protect him! He will enter this life with fears remaining from that event, such as the fear of loud noises. You must protect him closely and help him overcome these fears." The very instant after I absorbed the complete message, the birth began.

After the excitement of the day passed and I had a chance to sit down and reflect on what had happened, I wrote down the message so I would never forget it. It occurred to me as I wrote the note that, even though I faintly remembered the bombing of the barracks in Beirut from film clips on the news, I couldn't have remembered by myself in what year it had occurred. But I knew without a doubt that the message said "1983." I made a note to find out what year the explosion in Beirut had occurred. Later my research of old newspapers in the library confirmed the date as October 23, 1983.

Ever since that moment in the hospital, protecting and guiding Mark has been my life's mission. For the first time I really felt I had a purpose in my life. Today Mark is eight years old, and he is the best buddy I have ever had.

One evening when Mark was four, as I walked past his bedroom door, I heard him sobbing quietly. It was about eight-thirty in the evening and Mark was usually asleep by six-thirty or seven. I quietly opened the door a crack to look inside. Mark was on his bed, on his knees, sitting on his calves, with his head down, covering his face with his hands and sobbing. I had never seen him cry like that before. Normally when Mark cried, it was with his mouth wide open and face up in the air, making a very loud noise.

I quietly walked over, sat on the side of the bed, put my hand on his shoulder, and asked what was wrong. He was sobbing so deeply that at first he couldn't talk. I just rubbed his back softly and waited until he spoke. After a while he said between sobs, "All my friends are gone," shaking his head and gesturing with his hands. These were uncharacteristic mannerisms for Mark. His shoulders were slumped like he was carrying a very big burden, and he continued to look downward. Normally when Mark talks to you, he looks straight in your eyes. But now he was looking down at the bed, as if he were in a trance.

I asked, "What happened to them, Mark?"

He just shook his head sadly and said, "They're all gone."

I thought for a while, not sure what to say, while Mark continued to sob. Then I asked, "Where are your friends?"

He said, "They're under the rocks, the big rocks.

They're all gone." As soon as he said "big rocks" an image of television news reports of the Beirut barracks bombing popped into my mind. I remembered huge pieces of broken concrete piled up high, next to the remaining shell of a building.

I tried to think what to say to comfort Mark while he cried with his face in his hands. As I sat there I couldn't stop thinking that this was not the way a four-year-old child cries. Then, without my saying anything, Mark said, "I want to help my friends. They're all dying." Then he shook his head, put his face in his hands, and said through sobs, "But I can't, I can't."

I wanted to try to get him to talk through what he was feeling, hoping it would help him. But this whole episode had taken me so much by surprise, I really couldn't think what to say or do. Finally I asked, "Why can't you help them, Mark?"

Shaking his head sadly, he said, "Because all my power is gone. I can't move." I asked him where he was. He said, "I'm under the rocks too. All my power is gone." Then he started crying loudly, still with his face in his hands, saying, "I want to help my friends, but I can't. My power is all gone."

Not knowing what else to do, I just pulled Mark close to me and held his head next to my chest, rocking him to calm him down. He cried like I have never seen him cry before. After two or three minutes of intense crying, he finally calmed down a little and said softly, "They took me out from the rocks. They laid me down on one of the big rocks. They put me in a box and sent me back home." When he said that, I remembered the television image of the big concrete slab with bodies laid out on it and the scene on television of flag-draped coffins being unloaded from a cargo plane at an airport. I continued to hold Mark and rock him. He slowly stopped sobbing and, after a few minutes, fell asleep.

The words I have written above are the exact words that Mark used. I will remember every word of that conversation for the rest of my life. I remember thinking as he said the word *power* that he had no other way in his limited vocabulary to say that he had no life force left to help his friends. He had never heard the word *coffin*, so he called it a box. I also remember being impressed that his sole concern was helping his friends, even though he himself was crushed and dying—not a typical thought process for a four-year-old.

The next morning Mark was his typical energetic, optimistic, laughing self. There were no signs that he remembered anything about what had happened during the night. I never said anything to him about the episode, nor did he say anything to me.

Since he was very young, Mark has been intensely afraid of loud noises—just like the angel said he would be. As a toddler, any sudden loud noise would bring a look of absolute terror to his face and he would run into my arms. He still tells me he is afraid of loud noises and he will avoid any situation which he thinks could cause a sudden loud noise. When I read in your book, *Children's Past Lives,* about your son's memories of dying on a battlefield that were spontaneously triggered by the sounds of the fireworks, I understood what you went through. I really identified with the feelings you described as you held your son and realized the trauma he had experienced in his other life.

Mark had only one more episode, about a year later when he was five. It was triggered by a high fever, but otherwise was exactly the same, almost word for word. He sobbed uncontrollably, frustrated that he couldn't help his dead friends under the rocks because his power was gone. He died and was sent home in a box. After that last episode he never said anything again, and I have never asked him about it.

Parents need to understand the psychic wounds these precious souls bring with them, and the love they need to heal those wounds. If I had not heard the message of the angel in the delivery room, I wouldn't have had a clue to what Mark was talking about. And, like so many parents, I might have responded to Mark's pain by merely telling him to calm down and go to sleep.

I often think about Mark saying they put him in a box and sent him back home. It occurs to me that somewhere in the United States there is an empty room in some sad family's house with mementos of a young boy's life: pictures of a handsome boy in a baseball or football uniform, a picture of the boy in a marine uniform, and maybe some medals hanging on a plaque. I wish I could somehow tell that family that their son is now a strong, handsome, intelligent little boy, and that I will be taking good care of him.

# Chapter 9

## *A Second Chance*

*Although the doctors kept telling me Brent couldn't hear me or understand anything I was saying, I leaned down to his ear and spoke softly to him. I told him I would miss him more than anything in the world if he had to go. I told him never to forget that I loved him. Brent squeezed my finger and one tear dropped from the corner of his eye. He died two hours later.*

When someone close to you dies, there can be so many causes for regret, especially if the death was sudden and there was no time for good-byes, *I love you*s, or reconciliation. It can be particularly difficult if you needed to repair a relationship, to forgive or be forgiven, but hadn't found the right moment or the courage to do so. The finality of death appears to cut off any chance to fix the past.

And so it seemed to Beverly Kornik, whose story fills this entire chapter. Beverly was a teenage mother who badly mistreated her young son. Before she could mend their troubled relationship, he died suddenly. But through the miracle of family return, Beverly was blessed to be the mother of the very soul she had wronged before. She was truly given a second chance to redeem her past through her love and devotion for this new child.

You will notice that many elements of family return introduced in earlier chapters come together in Beverly's story. They include a birthmark, after-death communication, an announcing dream, telltale behaviors, and statements. They're all here.

You will also notice that Beverly's story is in many ways similar to Kathy Luke's—both mothers were reunited with a son they had lost to death. There is, however, an important difference. Kathy's is the story of *continuing* a relationship temporarily interrupted by death; reincarnation brings her together again to resume and deepen their love. Beverly's is the story of *changing* the relationship with her son and erasing destructive patterns from the past; reincarnation gives her the opportunity to correct her errors. Both are illustrations of how, as one soul travels its course through a single lifetime, another can weave in and out, bringing extraordinary spiritual lessons of forgiveness, mercy, and love.

## Guilt and Regrets

A woman approached me after a lecture I gave at the ARE (the Edgar Cayce Foundation) in Virginia Beach. She told me her friend Beverly was disappointed she couldn't make it to the conference, because she really needed to talk to me about her sons. Her firstborn died in an auto accident at the age of nineteen, and now she thought he was back as her two-year-old. Would I be interested, at all, in talking to her? I said yes, I would be *very* interested in talking to her friend—could I have her phone number and address? I was excited to discover that she lived in New Jersey, only an hour's drive from my home. Perhaps I could interview her in person.

As it turned out, it wasn't easy getting in touch with Beverly. Geography had nothing to do with it. After playing phone tag for a couple of months, I finally reached her at work one day. She spoke softly, with a hint of nervousness in her voice, as she gave me only the barest outline of her story. I was completely drawn in. I asked if I could contact her again when she wasn't working. She was evasive at first, but then explained that she and her husband were on the verge of separating, and she preferred not to discuss any of this in front of him. She offered to meet me at a Denny's restaurant near her house. We picked a date and exchanged self-descriptions.

Getting a substantial new case is always thrilling. So I was eager to meet Beverly and get to the heart of her story. I arrived at the Denny's at the appointed time and we immediately spotted each other in the crowd. After we sat down, Beverly confessed she was nervous about our meeting. She explained she had put off calling me back because she wasn't ready to talk about the death of her son, or to reveal painful secrets about herself. She didn't know what I would think about her story. I assured her nothing she could say would shock me—I was accustomed to the unusual and I had been trained as a counselor.

We sank into our orange-cushioned booth in the restaurant. Before she started telling her story, Beverly pulled two photos from her purse and laid them on the table before me. They showed two boys who looked to be about two years old. The boys looked very much alike—especially their eyes. Beverly pointed, "This is my son, Brent, who died in 1992. This is my son Jesse, who was born in 1995. I believe they're the same . . . the same soul." I was struck by the utter reality of the images before me.

Our waitress came with a carafe of coffee and took our order. Beverly began her story in a soft, tentative voice. I had to lean forward and focus intently on her to screen out the many distractions around us.

I was just seventeen when I had Brent. I was totally unprepared for the responsibilities of parenthood. To make matters worse, he was an unhappy and colicky baby. He screamed and cried all the time. I just couldn't handle it! I was so young, I could barely take care of myself, let alone a baby. I'm ashamed to admit it, but sometimes when Brent cried, I would shake his crib and scream, "Shut up! Shut up!" There were times when I would force myself to walk out of the room and close the door behind me so I wouldn't hurt him.

To make matters worse, my marriage was really bad. Vince was an alcoholic. When he drank, he was very, very abusive. One night he came home stinking drunk. When he saw three-month-old Brent crawling across the floor, he kicked him like a ball, slamming him against the wall. He could have killed the baby right there, and I'm ashamed to say I didn't do a thing to protect him. When Brent was only a year old, his father pointed a loaded gun at his head. I was afraid to do anything against my husband because when he went into one of his drunken rages he was dangerous, and I didn't know how far he would go. But he wasn't the only one who was abusive. As Brent got older, whenever he did anything wrong, I would hit him. I was not a good mom.

I had another son, Scott, when Brent was five. After Scott was born, I took both boys and left Vince. I was a single mom for fifteen years. Their father pretty much vanished from the scene; he called on Christmas, that was all.

Brent idealized his absent father. That's what the psychologists said, anyway. Brent was very sad about the separation, and in spite of his father's abuse, he blamed me for everything that had happened. At the same time, I was overwhelmed with guilt for not protecting him from his father, and for all the bad treatment I had inflicted on him. I tried to explain to him that I had taken him and his brother away because their father was dangerous and would have hurt him more. We both went into counseling to get help sorting out all the anger.

When Brent was fourteen he really wanted to be with his father, who was then living in Germany. I said okay. Brent spent four years with his dad; when he was eighteen, he came back to live with me and Scott. While he was overseas with his dad, I married Bruce.

I had a lot of time to think about my relationship with Brent while he was away, and I know I matured a lot during those four years. I began to understand what I had done to him when he was young and the motivations for my inexcusable behavior. After he came home, I really wanted to begin healing our relationship. I told him how much I regretted the pain I had caused him before. I remember crying and crying and saying to him, "I'm sorry for all the mean things I did to you. I wish I could make it up to you now. I really do love you. I always wanted to be a good mom, but I wasn't able to. I was too young." Many times I told him how much I regretted what I had done. The last time I told him was the day before he died in August of 1992.

I remember in particular one Friday night around that time. I prepared Brent's favorite dinner. Roast beef. During dinner, he confided to me he was having terrifying nightmares. They were always the same: In the dreams, he was fighting fiercely for his life, but he could never see who he was fighting against. He was very troubled by these dreams and asked me what I thought. I just looked at him and said, "Well, honey, just never stop fighting."

But Brent had another interpretation of these dreams. He said he knew he wasn't going to live long. He was so sure, in fact, he took out a life-insurance policy on himself, even though he was only nineteen. We were at the beach that August, and I overheard him tell his brother that he was leaving him some money.

Beverly stopped talking for a moment and took a few bites of her breakfast. I didn't even remember the waitress bringing it. I looked down at my eggs and saw they had hardened into cold yellow blobs on my plate. But it didn't matter. I was so totally absorbed in Beverly's story, I wasn't hungry. I distractedly resurrected my limp toast with some grape jelly.

I could feel how difficult it was for Beverly to talk about such heart-wrenching stuff. Now I understood why she had been so reluctant to meet with me and spill her dark secrets. My stomach was knotted—not from the food, but from knowing what was coming next in Beverly's story. We both took a sip of coffee to brace ourselves.

Late at night, on August 25, 1992, the police called to tell me Brent had been in a serious car accident. He had hit a tree and was not expected to live. I remember the horror and numbness I felt as we drove to the hospital. I was in shock. I kept saying to myself, "This can't be happening. This can't be happening."

When I got to the hospital, the doctors explained to me that Brent had taken the impact of the crash on his forehead. They assured me that because of the severity of the injury, he had gone unconscious immediately upon impact and hadn't felt a thing. They said it was like a light switching off. His head had hit the steering wheel with such force that half his brain was already dead. They had to wire his jaw shut so they could place a respirator in his mouth. I don't even know why they did that, because he was so far gone. But I was glad they did. Because, when I got there, he was still alive—just barely.

Brent's fists were clenched tight, as if he were still gripping the steering wheel. I slipped my finger into his tight fist. All I could think about was our conversation the night before when I told him never to stop fighting. I knew he was fighting now, struggling to stay alive. Although the doctors kept telling me Brent couldn't hear me or understand anything I was saying, I leaned down to his ear and spoke softly to him. I told him how much I loved him. I told him I would miss him more than anything in the world if he had to go.

But it was okay if he had to go; that was his decision. I told him never to forget that I loved him.

I held on to those moments with everything I had. Even though the doctors said he couldn't hear me, Brent squeezed my finger and one tear dropped from the corner of his eye. He died two hours later. I was by his side.

## Spirals of Beautiful Light

We both paused to take a breath. Beverly was holding back her tears. She admitted that even after six years it was still very hard for her to talk about the accident. I nodded, holding back my own tears.

For just a moment I stepped out of our bubble of concentration and became aware of all the chatter and movement around us in the restaurant. I commented to Beverly that the waitress had given up on us. The waitress noticed us looking around and came over to offer us more coffee. We thanked her for her patience and promised we would leave her a generous tip for taking up this table for her whole shift.

Then Beverly took a deep breath and picked up her story where she had left off.

I was in shock for a long time. I didn't eat for two weeks. It was months before I could shed any tears. I went to his grave every day. Scott was devastated too, but he rallied and tried to comfort me.

There were moments during this time, though, when I knew Brent was with me. Those were the only peaceful moments I had. The first time was immediately after the accident. I went to the police station because I had to help fill out the accident report. My father and I were answering questions. At one point I just couldn't sit still any longer and had to go outside to get some fresh air. It was a beautiful day and I was alone.

Suddenly a beautiful light showered over me, spreading like an umbrella. I turned around and saw the tiniest twinkling lights all around me—they surrounded me. There was tremendous energy there. I reached out to touch this flowing spiral of light and my hand went right through the middle of it. I stood there amazed, because I knew it was Brent. I could feel him.

This happened at least a half-dozen times over the next couple of years. Brent randomly appeared to me in spirals of beautiful light. The light would engulf me, no matter where I was or what I was doing. It felt wonderful. I could feel his presence in the light, so I would talk to him and say, "I know you're here, Brent. I wish I could see you. I know you're happy and not in pain. It makes me so happy to know you're here." He would stay for only a short time, and then he would leave. After these encounters, I always felt calm and peaceful.

Once, almost two years after his death, he communicated with me in a different way. One evening I was alone in the kitchen fixing dinner when, quite suddenly, a familiar smell filled the room. There are many types of cologne, but this was clearly the smell of Jovan Musk, which had been Brent's and my favorite. When he was little, we used to play this little game of tag with it: he would put on the cologne and I would run after him pretending I was following the scent. When I caught him, we would hug and giggle together. After Brent died, I wouldn't let anyone wear that particular cologne. So when the scent came into the kitchen, I knew Brent was with me again. It lasted for only a couple of minutes, then it went away.

Time passed, but I wasn't healing at all. I felt that the pain of his death would stay with me forever. My grief was made thicker by all the guilt I felt for helping make Brent's short life so miserable. I also felt cheated because he was ripped away from me just as we were healing our relationship. It all made me feel so hopeless, I just wanted to die. Still, I looked for any reason to hang on.

At first, having another child was the furthest thing from my mind. It seemed out of the question, even though I was in a new marriage and still in my thirties. But as time went on, I realized having another child would give me reason to carry on. I went into therapy to look at my motives for wanting to have a baby. I wanted to do it for the right reasons. I knew I couldn't replace Brent, and I also knew I couldn't redeem myself for all of the bad things I had done to him just by having another child. All I knew was that I wasn't done loving, I wasn't done hugging.

I got pregnant in 1994 at the age of thirty-nine. It was the most god-awful pregnancy. I was sick and vomited the whole time. Everything about it was exactly like the pregnancy with Brent, even though it had been more than twenty years before. The strange thing was that my pregnancy with Scott had been totally different—calm and peaceful. But these two were both awful.

I read somewhere that during the third trimester of pregnancy a mother can experience the soul or spirit of the baby come into her. Something happened during my seventh month that makes me wonder now about that idea.

Even though Brent had communicated with me in different ways after he died, he had never visited me in my dreams. I've heard this sometimes happens with other parents whose children have died. I always wanted him to, but he never did.

One night, though, when I was seven months pregnant, I dreamed of Brent. He appeared to me in a big, clear, open space. He was walking toward me with a little boy in tow. As they approached, I kept my eyes fixed on Brent. I was aware that there was a little boy with him, but it really didn't register what he was doing there. No words were exchanged, but Brent smiled, and I smiled back. He came close, but didn't touch me. Then he spoke to me. Pointing to the little boy, he said, "Mom, this is for you." And that was it; then he was gone. I woke up immediately.

Of course I have dreams all the time. But this was different. It was so clear and real. I was also very conscious in this dream and felt like I was totally there with Brent. I was stunned by the vividness of the dream for a long time. Now, almost five years later, whenever I try to remember what Brent looked like, I think back to that dream. That's how real it was.

After the dream, Brent never made contact with me again. There were no more spirals of light, no smells, no dreams. Nothing. I really didn't give a thought to the little boy in the dream. There was too much else going on.

*Jesse*

Two months later, in June of 1995, Jesse was born. Jesse came out screaming. When the doctor handed him to me, I noticed a large strawberry birthmark covering most of his forehead. I remember thinking that this mark was interesting, because he was born cesarean, so there hadn't been the usual birth trauma to his head. But I didn't think anything more of it at the time.

After Jesse came home, he screamed and cried all the time. The doctors told me it was colic, but I noticed that he couldn't stand having his head down. That made him cry more. So we always had to keep him in an upright position until he fell asleep. Bruce and I would walk with him constantly, pacing with him in our arms. It was an extremely difficult and exhausting time for both of us. I took Jesse to specialists to find out what was wrong with his head. He was diagnosed with severe ear infections, and they concluded that the infections were causing the pain.

But I began to wonder. It was strange that Jesse was born with the birthmark and so much head pain. I thought back to Brent's accident and how he had taken the impact on his forehead. And Brent had screamed and cried for months after birth, just like Jesse. Was it just a coincidence? And that dream in which Brent was presenting the little boy to me. Was Brent trying to tell me something symbolically about that child?

And, Jesse looked exactly like Brent at that age— their faces, hair, eyes, and even their bodies were the same—although they had different fathers who don't look anything alike. With my middle son, Scott, whenever he smiled or deviled me, I could see his father in him. But Brent and Jesse resemble only each other—not me, and not their fathers. Sometimes I would reason, "Of course there are similarities—they're stepbrothers." But there seemed to be more to it than that.

I began to wonder if the connection between my sons could be explained by reincarnation, although I wasn't quite sure what it meant. Reincarnation was only an idea I had heard about, but I couldn't understand how it could relate to my life. I only knew there were these strange similarities between my two sons. Taken separately, they didn't mean a thing. But taken all together, they made me wonder if it could be possible that Brent was back. I was also careful not to jump to any conclusions because I knew how easy it would be for me to imagine this, or impose Brent's identity on Jesse. Of course I wanted my son back—if that was possible.

But as time went on, and Jesse's personality came out, more things happened that pointed to reincarnation, things I couldn't deny:

When Jesse first started talking, right after his first birthday, he pointed to a picture of Brent in our bedroom and yelled, "Me, me!" I explained to him that it was a picture of his brother, and that he looked very much like his brother. But again he insisted, "Me!" I tried to dismiss it. But then it happened again, a year or so later. We were looking at photos at my mother's. I was showing Jesse pictures of our wedding and of his older brother, Scott. When we got to an old picture of Brent as a baby, Jesse started yelling, "Me, Mommy, me!" He was so forceful about it.

When he was about eighteen months old, something else happened while we were visiting my mother. My mother has always been a heavy smoker. Brent hated her smoking, and he used to torment her about it. Every time she would light a match, he would jump up and blow it out. One day, when Jesse and I were at my mother's, we were rolling pool balls back and forth on the floor at each other. He had only been walking for a few months by that time. My mother started lighting a cigarette with her lighter. Immediately Jesse jumped up and ran over and blew out the lighter. We all just stopped dead. Brent was the only other person who ever did that. We didn't say anything in front of Jesse, but in our hearts we knew it was Brent. He didn't only do it that one time either, he did it a number of times after that.

## Looking for Something

Shortly after this, something else happened that really clinched it for me. We live in an older neighborhood with older apartment buildings and some houses. Jesse liked to play on a neighbor's swing set that was across the street from our building. One day, when he was around eighteen months old, I was pushing him on the swing. He jumped off and toddled into the backyard of the neighbor's house. I followed him. He kept walking like he knew where he was going and was looking for something. He went through the neighbor's yard and across the alleyway which ran along the back of the yard. He crossed the alleyway and stepped into the front yard of another house. Then he stopped in his tracks and just stared. He was staring at the apartment house where I had raised Brent. I had never taken him there before, and, from a toddler's perspective in walking distance, this was a world far from home. At that moment I was sure he was Brent returned. I knew it.

But I wanted to test him. I asked, "What are you doing there looking at that house?" He turned around, smiled, and led me down a driveway to another neighbor's yard and went straight to their swing set. He knew his way around, and he knew exactly where to find that swing set. That was the place where Brent used to swing when he was little. In that moment each of us knew the other knew the truth. It's hard for me to share this with anyone, because it sounds so strange.

That was a wonderful moment I will never forget. That's when I knew I could accept that Brent was back again. I knew he was back here to start over and enjoy his life more this time. Slowly I understood that knowing this was helping to soften my pain and lift some of the guilt I've been carrying around for so long. Once I realized this was true, other parts of Jesse's personality and some of his behaviors began to fit together into a complete picture.

Brent had been very athletic. He played soccer, baseball, basketball—anything that involved a ball. But he had a knee injury that prevented him from playing sports seriously. Now Jesse is getting a really early start with sports. Since he was a little baby he was always fascinated with balls. He always has to have balls around him—big balls, little balls. In fact, he learned to walk by playing soccer. As he got older, he would kick the ball farther and farther. So by the time he was walking, he was kicking balls quite a distance. Now, at age three, he's as good with a ball as a seven- or eight-year-old. He could hit a baseball clear across a field at age two. Even my husband is amazed by his natural ability.

There's another quirky thing about Jesse. From the time he was able to sit up in a stroller and point to what he wanted, he would point to hats. Now, at age three, this boy must have at least three dozens hats in the house. He has every color, every shape of hat. No matter where he goes, if he sees a hat, he has to have it. He wears them all the time. I've never known any other kids at that age who insisted on wearing a hat. Except Brent. He *always* wore hats. He didn't only wear baseball caps, which many young boys wear, but any hat. He loved hats, just like Jesse does now. If it weren't for all of the other things, I would write this off as coincidence. But it's part of the whole thing.

Now, at age four, certain memories of Brent's life seem to bleed through into Jesse's mind. Sometimes they'll pop out because something will remind him of an event in Brent's life. For example, just recently, there was a story on the radio about a three- or four-year-old who set his house on fire and was severely burned. This story triggered fear in me. So, as I was folding the laundry, I sat Jesse on the dryer and explained to him what that little boy had done, how he had gotten hurt, and how important it is not to play with fire.

Jesse nodded and said, "Yeah, Mommy. Like that time when our bathroom was on fire and I had to save my brother."

I stopped folding, turned to him, and gasped, "*What* did you say?"

He said, "When I lived in my *other* house." I was stunned, but tried to maintain my composure. I said, "Where did you live?" He said, "Down near Grandma's."

When Brent and Scott were little, for a while we lived in an apartment within walking distance of my mother's. One day the electricity went off when the two boys were in the tub. At the time Brent was eight and Scott was three. I told them not to move while I ran to get some candles. I lit the candles and told them to stay in the tub while I got their pajamas. Well, no sooner had I walked out of the bathroom than Scott stepped out of the tub and knocked a candle into the trash can. The room went up in a blaze and Brent grabbed his brother and pushed him out of the bathroom. This all happened in a few seconds. Brent really had rescued his brother.

So I acknowledged what Jesse was saying. "That was a very scary time for us, wasn't it?" He agreed, but then just stopped talking about it. That was it. The memory just came and went.

There have been so many instances when Jesse will do something, say something, or we'll see a mannerism that stands out as being from Brent. When I look into his eyes, sometimes I see and feel Brent there. But Jesse is Jesse—he's his own person. I don't know if Brent and Jesse came from heaven as two separate souls or one. It is a mystery. But I feel that now they are one soul joined, melded together.

Jesse seems so anxious to begin again where he left off. He is always in a rush to grow up. He can't wait to get up in the morning and do things big kids do. I remind him he has plenty of time. Occasionally, that gets him to slow down and be content with little boys' toys.

## Soul Repair

Having brought her story up to the present, Beverly paused, and then excused herself for a minute and left the table. For the first time in more than an hour I looked around. I noticed the restaurant was filling up with lunch customers eating hamburgers. Our patient and understanding waitress had cleared away our plates a long time ago and left us alone. I didn't see her anywhere; another waitress was serving her tables, but hadn't bothered us.

With the spell broken for a moment, I had a chance to think about what was happening. I had worried at first that Beverly might be too guarded and ashamed to reveal her true feelings. But as she became more comfortable with me, it was obvious that she was digging deep and trying to express how she felt through the entire experience. Her tone lightened when she talked about Jesse and all the similarities to Brent. I could sense she was in the process of healing.

She had finished relating the events of her story, but I felt there was more I wanted to know and more she had to say. I wanted to probe a bit more and ask her what this all meant to her. Had her prayers been answered? Did she feel absolved of her past by knowing her son was back?

When she returned to the table, I came right out and asked her, "What does it mean to you that Brent is back?"

Beverly looked thoughtful for a moment, then began to speak. Clearly, she had given this question some thought before.

I believe God has a twofold plan for me. The first part is for me to overcome my guilt for what happened. For twenty years I believed I hadn't loved Brent and that's why I treated him the way I did. Now I realize I was just too young to have a baby, and he suffered because of it.

The second part of the plan is to give Brent a chance to live again. He was so young and he left this world so violently. When Brent squeezed my finger and the tear fell down his cheek in the hospital, I believe it was his way of saying he would come back. It was his promise. He had so many things he wanted to do, he was so alive. But his life was cut short by an accident. Even though it was terrible, I believe it was all God's plan. He has given Brent back to me so he can have a better life and I can share in it. He'll be able to have all the happiness he should have had the first time around. I *know* this is true.

If Jesse had rejected me, or if he had given me a hard time as a way to get back at me for what I did in the past, I wouldn't blame him. But I guess my apologies and regrets were heard, and he's forgiven me. I told Brent repeatedly how I regretted what I had done. During the last few months of Brent's life, almost every day, I would cry and say to him, "I'm sorry for all the mean things I've done to you. I wish I could make it up to you, because I do love you. I always wanted to be a good mom, but I didn't know how."

We still have a lot of mending and healing to do. Everything is not automatically right just because he's back as Jesse. I still have trouble letting go of Brent, even though I know he's back. The feelings of grief and guilt don't just disappear in knowing it. I still have to work through my guilt by being a better mother this time and letting this new child grow and become his own person.

Occasionally, some of our old patterns of behavior appear, and we both recognize them. We also see that they need to be changed. For example, something happened recently that gave me quite a jolt. Jesse has been playing with other kids and is picking up some bad habits from them. A few times he's stuck out his tongue at me and given me a raspberry. I don't like that. It's very disrespectful. So I've been correcting him, patiently asking him not to do it. But the other night he stuck out his tongue and did it again. I gently smacked him on the face—not hard—and said, "Don't do that. It's disrespectful." That's the first time I've spanked him or hit him in any way. Jesse burst into tears and cried and cried. I let him cry for a couple of minutes, then I picked him up and said, "Okay, why are you so upset?"

He stopped crying and looked me straight in the eye and said, "Don't hit me, Mom. Don't hit me anymore *like you used to*!" That struck me so deeply, I thought I was going to be sick.

So you see, healing is an ongoing process. Everything is not automatically right just because he's back. I still have to work through things—some of the same things I did wrong before. But it's different this time. Jesse is a much happier spirit, with enough awareness to correct me when I need it. And I'm a different mother than I was twenty-five years ago. I'm much more attentive, caring, and willing to look at my mistakes and change. I thank God every day that I have a second chance to show Jesse what kind of mom I can be.

It's strange, but I hardly go to the cemetery anymore to visit Brent's grave. Only on special occasions. Sometimes I feel guilty about this, because I used to go all the time before Jesse was born. I went every week. Since I've had Jesse, I don't feel the need to go down there.

I was deeply moved by Beverly's story. I admired her courage in facing her past actions and accepting the truth that her son returned to her. As joyous as it is to have her son back, it also means she must face, literally and in a most profound way, her mistakes with him in the past. I understand what an incredible gift and blessing this is for her soul—to be given a second chance. If she can conquer her old demons by loving her son now, she will free herself from a burden that would have tormented her all her life, and probably beyond. She won't have to wait for an uncertain reunion with her son in the afterlife to make amends. She can do it now. This, to me, sums up the miracle of reincarnation.

I asked her: "Beverly, when I share your story in my next book, I know it will move and inspire a lot of people. What do you want to tell people about what this experience means for your life? What are your final thoughts?"

I would tell people that having a reincarnated child is, honestly, a wonderful, enlightening experience. Oh, but I wouldn't wish the death and guilt in my life on anyone. Some lives have many trials and tribulations, while other people seem to glide through life on a surfboard. I've been pulled through kicking and screaming! For people like me, with the hard lives, I want them to realize that life goes on. It just goes on.

But, you know, in a way our lives are not our own. I believe they are planned out before we even get here, and in a lot of ways we are guided. When God decides you need to learn certain things, He shows you by leading you through the experience—whatever it takes for people to learn how to love.

I don't really know what the word *reincarnation* means, but I can say that I believe, without a shadow of a doubt, that the spirit lives on. And the spirit goes through life to experience as many things as it can in order to learn how to love. We are here to love so we can move on to a higher plane and be closer to God. That's the whole reason we're here, and why we come back after we die.

In a million years I could never find enough words of gratitude to God for sending Brent back to me. I've had so many other things go wrong in my life, and I made so many mistakes. I would never have thought I deserved such a blessing. If only other people with pain in their lives could experience this—being given the opportunity to make things right—they would see what a total miracle and gift from God this is.

I have learned, though, that I have to be very careful who I share this with. My religious girlfriends think I'm crazy. They've told me there is no such thing as reincarnation, it's the devil's work and an abomination against God. That's so naive. How can anyone be so close-minded to this beautiful power? It's so sad they're missing such a miracle of God's love and mercy.

# Chapter 10

*Soul Weaving*

*Here was this incredible wisdom coming from a two-year-old barely out of diapers. How could I deny what happened? It was so real, and nothing a two-year-old could come up with in his imagination. It went far deeper than that—far deeper than anything I've ever been taught or could imagine.*

Up to this point we've taken a narrow, close-up look at the phenomenon of family return. We've focused on the children with the memories and on the reactions of parents and other members of the family. And we've seen how the families' lives and beliefs were changed by the experience.

Yet there is more to gain from studying these stories. If we step back to get a wider view and look at all the implications, we see that family return holds far-reaching spiritual lessons for all of us—whether or not we have experienced it directly in our own family.

One of the lessons is that love has the power to transcend death. We see this in the cases where a soul chooses, for reasons of love, to be reborn to the family it recently left behind. We see in so many other cases that the bonds of love are not severed at death, but continue in a new relationship in another life. "True love never dies" is a sentimental cliché we hear in pop songs and poetry, but now we see it's literally true.

People I talk to who have witnessed reincarnation in their families tell me it changed how they look at death. They confess they are no longer afraid of the *finality* of death. They know—because they've seen it with their own eyes—that it is *not* the absolute end of existence, but is simply the end of one phase of a continuous cycle of life.

For example, when Kathy Luke lost her young son to death, she expected it to be final. But when she realized seventeen years later that his soul had returned to her as a new child, her worldview changed and she lost her fear of death. This is how she described the change:

> The way I see it now, our lives move in a circle, and strong relationships stay in the circle. I believe because it works this way that, when my time is done, I will be back again with those I love. It's reassuring to know this. Before, I was never comfortable with dying. *Death doesn't bother me now.* I know I will be back and reconnect with those I love.

We can take comfort in what Kathy and the others have discovered when it is our turn to grieve. Seeing life as part of a continuous cycle takes the despair out of death. Understanding that the soul does not die can be a balm for our grief.

Same-family reincarnation changes how we feel about our *own* deaths. Knowing that death is not the ultimate end—that we will be given many more chances on Earth to learn, to grow, to fulfill our purpose and be with the ones we love—helps us face the fact that some day we too will die. And, as so many mystical traditions teach, when we lose our fear of death, we gain a new perspective on how to live.

## Intersections of Purpose

Any one instance of same-family reincarnation is a simple weaving of one soul in and out of the lives of the family it left behind. And if it can happen once, it can happen any number of times, creating a pattern of familiar souls weaving through each other's lives, intersecting at different points in time. The fabric of relationship grows as souls travel through future generations and beyond the immediate family. With each new incarnation the soul may intersect with former friends, lovers, even enemies who touched it at significant moments in a past life. It branches out to intersect with souls it has never encountered before on its journey through time. Extend this image to its limits and we can envision an infinitely rich fabric of intertwining relationships beginning countless lifetimes ago and stretching countless lifetimes into the future.

If every soul has an ultimate and higher purpose, then at each intersection there is an overlapping of plans. At each intersection we come together with other souls for the mutual opportunity to grow and evolve into more loving, compassionate, and forgiving human beings.

At some of these intersections we find our soul mates—those with whom we have shared profoundly positive bonds in the past. We usually think of a soul mate as a lover or a spouse, but it can be anyone—a child who brightens our life, a teacher who points the way, or a dear friend who understands us implicitly. These are the souls who affect us so deeply that they take a prominent place in our hearts for our whole life.

We might also encounter difficult, challenging, and even dangerous relationships at these intersections. An abusive spouse, a boss who fires us, or a double-crossing adversary might be an unwitting teacher of painful but necessary lessons. Difficult relationships like these sometimes force us to change direction, stand up for ourselves, or find strength and inner resources we didn't know we had. Though it may be hard to believe at the time, from a cosmic perspective there is love and intention behind these difficult meetings too.

This purposeful weaving of souls through time is more than a beautiful, abstract image. It's something we can feel when it happens. We feel it in our hearts when we meet a soul mate for the first time. We *get it* when we look into the eyes of a newborn and are floored by the old soul looking back at us. These are luminous moments of recognition when we feel the truth of our connectedness to all souls and get a glimpse of the cosmic meaning of intersecting lives.

Kathy Luke felt it. Drawing from her incredible experience with James and Chad, she attempted to describe it:

> It feels like Chad and I have always been there for each other. I'm not sure how to put it, but to say that we've been together once or twice in other lives is not quite

accurate. It goes much deeper than that. I feel we've always been together. The feelings I have for him are like the feeling you get when holding a baby—that calmness and peacefulness. But it goes much deeper.

Once we understand that any significant relationship in our lives could be a continuing thread from the past, we know to be alert for clues to its deeper meaning. We can try to discern the reasons a particular person has come into our lives. We can try to make the most of the connection, seeing it as an opportunity to learn whatever it is we need to learn from the relationship this time around. Even if we can't discover the reasons, just knowing that any relationship might be an intersection of spiritual purpose opens our eyes to the potential significance of even the smallest encounters that weave across our path.

Sarah Holden (from the "Mother Switching" chapter) began looking at all of her relationships differently after she realized that her abusive mother had returned as her son Miles. She reflects:

> When I look at people now I wonder what they went through in the past and why they're back. Especially with the people I'm close to, I wonder if we've had a connection before in another life and why we are brought together again. I want to make the most of our experience together.

## Fear of Karma

Everyone, I believe, has made at least one regrettable and seemingly irreversible mistake in his or her life.

Another hopeful lesson in the family return stories is that we have the opportunity to correct mistakes and make amends—if not in this lifetime, then in another.

Again, Sarah Holden shares what she learned from her experience:

> Because of my experiences with Miles, I realize that if we don't finish things by the time we die or if we make mistakes with people, we get another chance to rectify things. Miles has taught me it's never too late to make things right. There's no point in beating yourself up if things go wrong with someone, because you get another go at it.

It is significant that Sarah Holden's mother in her reincarnation as Miles did not have to suffer the same abuse as she had inflicted on her own family before she died. Instead, she was given an opportunity through love, not punishment, to grow beyond the person she was before.

I believe one of the reasons Westerners resist reincarnation is that they have trouble with the idea of karma. Some object on intellectual grounds that it's too simplistic and fatalistic. Some are simply afraid of it. They've heard karma associated with the principle "you reap what you sow" and fear that if they return to another life, they will be forced to face all their former actions and suffer in kind for every hurt they ever inflicted. They resist such a system that leaves no room for free will, mercy, or change.

Cases like Sarah Holden's, though, show that karma is not so strict and unforgiving. There is much more creativity, grace, and flexibility than we realize in the process that guides us to our next life.

One story, of a two-year-old's past life vision, changed my understanding of karma more than anything else I had heard up to that time. It taught me how the soul has many options in correcting and balancing past actions, solutions that go far beyond simple cause and effect. It opened my eyes to how merciful divine justice can be, and how it is available to any of us, even a murderer.

This account from Sandra Poole is taken from a phone interview. She explains what happened one night to her son, Alex:

Alex had just turned two when this happened. I was tucking him into bed and he was beginning to doze off to sleep. Suddenly he bolted up in his bed, seemed to focus on something on the opposite wall of his room, and began screaming and crying. His sudden outburst caught me totally off guard because I couldn't see anything that could have triggered it. My mother rushed in from the other room when she heard Alex wailing.

We asked him, "What's wrong, what's wrong?"

Alex sobbed, "The man, the man. He's got a gun, Mom, and he's going to shoot me."

I tried to hold him and reassure him there was no man in his bedroom and he was safe, but I couldn't get through to him. He was so scared he tried to crawl backward into his headboard. He continued to wail and cry, fixated on something in front of him only he could see. My mother and I kept repeating, "What's wrong? What's wrong?"

He cried, "He shot me."

Hoping I could figure out what was going on, I joined him in his vision. I said, "He shot you? Are you dead?"

He said, "Not yet. That's why he's getting the knife. Oh, Mama, he's cutting my throat." He screamed and struggled and held his throat for what seemed like a couple of minutes.

My mother and I were completely baffled. We held him, but he still didn't seem to be aware of us. I was beside myself with worry. Here was my sweet little two-year-old totally absorbed in this horrible scene. I was desperate to figure out where this was coming from. I quickly scanned in my mind all the movies he had seen to recall if he had been exposed to these scary images before—he's only two and I knew everything he had seen. But I was drawing a blank.

As Alex continued to sob and wail, I tried to get more information from him: "What does the room look like?"

"It has wood walls."

"Do you drive a car, truck, or horse?" I asked, trying to put this into some time frame.

"I have a horse."

I was beginning to think he might be remembering something from the past—maybe from another life. At the same time I was trying to snap him out of it. My mother and I shook him gently every few minutes, saying, "Come on, Alex. Look at me. There's no man. You're here, safe with us." But he didn't respond at all. He kept crying and staring at the same spot on the wall.

Then, after about twenty minutes, his state suddenly changed. It was as if someone had flipped a switch. He quickly relaxed and settled down into the bed, and strangely enough, he was beaming with the most beautiful smile I've ever seen. He wasn't focusing on the wall anymore, but he was still in some sort of trance.

Calmly, and with a mature tone to his voice that totally surprised me, he said, *"Oh, it's going to be okay. He's going to be my son and I'll teach him not to hurt people and not to shoot guns. And I'll teach him to love instead of hurt."*

After he said that, Alex looked very content and totally relaxed. With a big smile on his face he began to close his eyes. I said, "Okay, Alex, why don't you just go to sleep." My mother and I tucked him in, and he went right to sleep, the smile still on his face. That was the whole thing. That was it.

My mother and I retreated to the living room. Tears were streaming out of her eyes. We sat and hugged each other and both said over and over again, "Oh, my God! That was so beautiful!" I was touched more deeply by this than anything I had ever experienced before. I was so glad my mother was there too as a second witness to this extraordinary lesson and to remind me later that it really happened.

I've always been open in a cerebral sort of way to the concept of reincarnation. My attitude used to be that reincarnation might be true and it might not, but since I didn't have any personal experience with it, I didn't know. I'm a skeptical, doubting Thomas by nature, and I don't embrace an idea unless I can see concrete evidence to back it up. Yet here was this incredible wisdom coming from a two-year-old barely out of diapers. How could I deny what happened? It was so real, and nothing a two-year-old could come up with in his imagination—it went far deeper than that, far deeper than anything I've ever been taught or could imagine.

I've always had a real problem with the Christian doctrine of hell because it has no compassion. I believe that most people who do bad things come from harsh backgrounds or are traumatized in some way when they're young, and the deck is stacked against them. I come from a long line of fundamentalists—exorcism and snake-handling types—who accuse anyone who does a bad thing of being possessed by Satan or demons. I think that's wrong. That type of judgment takes away a person's free will—it denies that they are an individual with the ability to make their own decisions. It damns them without looking at the circumstances that led the person to make a bad choice.

Yet the level of forgiveness Alex spoke of is so overwhelming and wonderful! Before he spoke of this solution to the past life wrong committed by that murderer, my understanding of karma had been "you reap what you sow." So I would have thought if my son and that man had a karmic debt to work out, they'd meet on some battlefield and Alex would get back at him by doing to him exactly what the man did to him in the past life. But the solution to have him come back as Alex's son, to be father to the man, shows a much greater wisdom than that. It was much more compassionate than simple retribution and punishment.

I can see how having to be a father to his own murderer would help my son evolve spiritually by forcing him to give compassion so deeply to the soul who took something so great from him. At the same time, how humbling it would be for the murderer's soul to accept that gift. My two-year-old, more than anyone else, has taught me about redemption, hope, and the true meaning of compassion.

The next morning Alex had absolutely no memory of what happened the night before or the man with the gun and the knife. He showed no effects from the experience. He was fine. In fact he was more than fine: That night marked the end of his asthma. Since he was five months old he had been taking prescription medication for his asthma, and I remember clearly the last time he needed a treatment was the night before he saw this past life. After a couple of months I realized he was healed and the medication was gathering dust on the shelf. My mother and I were completely changed by what we saw that night, and apparently Alex was too.

Alex's story opened my heart to a higher, more compassionate standard of forgiveness. It demonstrates that the universal laws governing reincarnation are more unpredictable and benevolent than I had imagined. Reincarnation does not trap a soul in a rigid cause-and-effect cycle, but provides the keys for rehabilitation through a change in circumstance. A thief in one life can be a philanthropist in the next.

Even if we make horrible mistakes and hurt others terribly, we are not eternally condemned to a flaming, Dantean hell, and we do not have to suffer for our misdeeds through a strict and literal "eye for an eye" system of retribution. Instead, it appears that justice and balance can be achieved creatively, with infinite flexibility. The beauty of reincarnation is that we are given as many opportunities as we need to learn and grow beyond our human failings.

## Looking for the Light

I have one last story to tell before I bring this book to a close. It dramatizes a theme running through many stories in the previous chapters.

The theme is belief—or to be precise, how people's prior beliefs can affect their ability to see a case of reincarnation in their family when it happens. What amazes me is what a big difference a small change in attitude can make. Staying open, even a little bit, can make the difference between seeing a case of reincarnation or missing it completely.

In earlier chapters, I described the process parents typically go through as their child's past life memories open their eyes to reincarnation. If, before it happened to them, you had asked these parents if they believed in reincarnation, many would have answered, "No," or "I'm skeptical." But when their children began to show signs of a past life, they withheld their judgment, watched, and evaluated. They maintained an "it might be this, or it might be that" attitude throughout, and they didn't cut off their child when he or she began to talk about another life. By staying open and nonjudgmental, these parents were rewarded with a miracle that enriched their lives and enhanced their spiritual awareness.

What you do not see described in this book are all the times when parents flatly refuse to entertain the possibility for reincarnation even when it happens to their own children. Their staunch belief that "we only live once" precludes them from seeing the evidence right under their noses. This fixed attitude can come from their loyalty to a religious creed or to the belief that anything not proven by science can't be real. So if their young child begins to speak of "when I was big before," they scold and silence her, and the case is nipped in the bud.

Yet I know these cases exist because I hear from frustrated relatives on the sidelines—aunts, uncles, or grandparents—who see clear signs of reincarnation in their little niece, nephew, or grandchild. They are convinced of it, but the child's parents forbid any discussion of past lives and may accuse the well-meaning relative of encouraging the child in "this nonsense." The relatives stay quiet to preserve peace in the family, but they e-mail me and ask for my advice. I confirm that what they are seeing is possible, but without the parents' consent I am as helpless as they are to get involved any further.

I also know it happens because I hear from adults who remember having past life memories as a child. Many can pinpoint the moment when they were "shushed" or ridiculed into keeping their memories to themselves. Some remember that all it took was one remark or one laugh from an adult to shut them down. Hearing from these people has taught me how easily some children learn to stay quiet about anything the parents won't believe. Despite the discouragement, these adults never forgot the vivid memories of another life. They contact me to thank me for finally confirming what they felt was true all along.

Clearly, the children lose out when they aren't allowed to express their past life memories. And so do the parents. They not only miss the joy of welcoming home a beloved relative, they also miss the opportunity to experience reincarnation directly and gain a new perspective on the life of the soul.

Now for the last story. This came to me in an e-mail from Claire, a mother living in a small Indiana town. Because she remained open (with a nudge from her mother) to what her son was trying to tell her, she witnessed a miracle. But then, with whom could she and her mother share their secret?

One day my two-year-old son Derek and I were visiting my mother, and we were all baking peanut-butter cookies together. Out of the blue, as he was "helping" me place the cookie dough on the greased pan, Derek informed us, "My *other* mommy used to make this kind of cookies too."

A little doubtful, I said, "Your *other* mom? What . . ."

Before I could say anything else, my mother nudged me and said, "Shhh!" She didn't want me to stop the flow of what he was saying.

He said, "My other mother, *Dorsey.*" I was waiting for him to say more, but instead he started talking about how many cookies he was going to eat.

I was a little shocked by this remark. But my mother, who had read a great deal about reincarnation before Derek was born, told me he was probably remembering a previous life, and we should allow him to talk without denying or suppressing him. I wasn't so sure, but I was willing to wait and see if he said anything else interesting.

I didn't have to wait long. Over the next year Derek spoke often of his other mother, "Dorsey" (we assumed he meant "Dorothy" but couldn't pronounce the *th* sound). He added other details and talked about his brother Matt and a sister, but he couldn't remember the sister's name. He made these remarks about his other family at random times. He would often compare what I did with what Dorsey used to do. For example, once when he was sick and I was putting a cool washcloth on his forehead, he told me approvingly, "Dorsey used to do that too when I was sick."

He got stuck on one particular memory of his other mother. He said that whenever he went out at night, his mother would leave the outside light on for him.

He specifically described how the light hung off the side of the garage. He added that his mother would turn on the outside light and wave to him from a little round window on the side porch. He repeated this several times. I thought this was odd since we didn't have a round window or a light like that at our house.

During this time my mother admitted she had a feeling about Derek, and she would often say, "I *know* him." I would laugh and tell her, "Of course you know him, he's your grandson!"

But she would say, "No, it's something else, something more. I *know* him from somewhere . . ." But she couldn't put her finger on it. Since she was a believer in reincarnation, she decided they must have known each other in another life long ago.

Soon after Derek turned three, I was driving through a part of town I rarely visited and Derek was in the back in his car seat. Suddenly I heard him squeal, "There it is! That's my house! That's where my other mom is!!"

I stopped the car. He was practically jumping out of his car seat as he pointed to a house on the corner with a detached garage. He was *very* excited and kept repeating, "My house! There's my house!"

I turned the car onto the side street and stopped again to get a better look at the garage. And there they were: the light hanging off the side of the garage and the round window on the side porch, exactly as he had described it. I thought about all the times he talked about his mother waving good-bye from that window and keeping the outside light on for when he came home. But now the light wasn't on.

When Derek saw that the light wasn't on, he was greatly disturbed and upset. He cried, "Why isn't the light on for me?" Then he pointed to the window. "That's where my other mom waved good-bye to me *the last time I left home*."

I didn't know what to say or do. I could imagine Derek remembering a past life, but I couldn't imagine we had found the actual house where he had lived before in our town. Maybe it looked like his other house—but to actually be *the* house? I found it hard to believe. The thought entered my mind to knock on the door. But what would I say? It would sound too crazy. So I started the car. As I was driving away, I looked in the rearview mirror at Derek. He was slumped in his car seat looking so very sad and lost, as if someone had just died. He started to cry softly and wouldn't talk to me until we got home.

A few days later I mentioned this incident to my mother, telling her how the house, the light on the garage, and the round window matched everything Derek had said before. I described Derek's strong reaction when he saw that one particular house and his comment about the *"last time I left home"* and his utter disappointment that the light wasn't on for him.

As I talked my mother grew uncharacteristically still. When I finished, she asked me the exact location of the house. As soon as I told her which corner it was on, she let out the loudest, most shocked sound I've ever heard come out of her.

After she caught her breath, she exclaimed, "Do you realize who lived there?"

I told her I had no idea.

"My cousin Ted once lived in that house with his mother, Doris, a brother Matt, and his sister Becky. Ted was killed in an automobile accident in 1971, just one week after he returned from fighting in Vietnam."

Now I was shocked too. I had never heard of my mother's cousin Ted or his death.

She told me all about him. She and Ted were very close—they were about the same age and had gone to school together. She added that Ted had a best friend all through grade school and high school and the two boys went to Vietnam together. After coming home from the war, this friend married and had children. One of this friend's children is now my husband! So Ted's best friend is now Derek's grandfather!

Aunt Doris moved far away from our Indiana town many years ago, and my mother lost touch with her. Over the next few weeks we debated whether we should try to find Aunt Doris and tell her about Derek and his past life memory. The whole time my mother knew her, she was a faithful churchgoer and fond of quoting Bible verses. We reasoned that it was unlikely she believed in reincarnation, and she would think we were crazy if we approached her with this. But should we tell her anyway? After considering all of the possible outcomes, we decided it was best not to risk upsetting an elderly woman.

We decided not to bring it up with my husband's father, Ted's best friend, either. We know he doesn't believe in reincarnation and would definitely think we were crazy. He and Derek have such a close and loving relationship, we decided we didn't want to say anything that might disturb it. Strangely enough, from the time Derek was two or three he would ask his grandfather questions about war and fighting. He specifically wanted to know if there were other ways to die besides being shot. He was really eager to get detailed information about dying and would carry on adult conversations with his grandfather, which was bizarre to see because Derek was only three at the time. Also from very early on, Derek was absolutely terrified of fireworks. Looking back on it, I wonder if his questions about war and his fear of fireworks had something to do with his combat days in Vietnam.

After that day when three-year-old Derek saw the house, he didn't mention his other mom or the house or the light again. Now he is ten and remembers only what we have told him about his memories of the garage light and "Dorsey." His own images of his past life as Ted have faded completely.

After seven years it still bothers me that my mother and I can't share our secret with others in our family. I almost picked up the phone on a couple of occasions to find Aunt Doris and tell her, but changed my mind each time because the chances are small it would do any good. And I still think if Derek's grandfather knew that Derek is the reincarnation of Ted, his closest friend all through childhood, it might deepen their relationship even more—not to mention change my father-in-law's ideas about death. My mother and I can see it's part of a greater plan for them to be together again and enjoy their special friendship once more. But since he doesn't believe in reincarnation and we know it's not safe even to broach the subject with him, we just keep it to ourselves. I often think, though, wouldn't it be wonderful if he and Aunt Doris could see the miracle that my mother and I see.

There is no way of knowing if Claire and her mother made the right decision not to look up Doris and tell her of their discovery. I believe they probably did, given what they knew from the past about Doris and her strong religious beliefs. (They didn't have to guess about the grandfather, and that probably added to their justification for not telling Doris.) It was likely that Doris would only have been hurt and offended by their challenge to her beliefs with their "impossible" claim that her dead son was back.

I can imagine how sensitive she would be to opening the wound of her son's death, even thirty years later. Losing a child is the worst thing that can happen to any mother, and the cruel timing of Ted's death must have made it even more unbearable for her. I imagine Doris waited endless, agonizing months for him to return from Vietnam. Then, just days after he finally came home to her, after the joy and profound relief that he was finally safe from the dangers of a faraway war, she got the dreadful call with the news that Ted had been killed in a car accident close to home.

Yes, Claire and her mother were probably right not to take the chance of upsetting Doris after all she had been through. But what if things had been different?

What if Doris were open to the possibility of reincarnation and they knew it, and they contacted distant relatives and got her phone number and called her? What would she feel when they described Derek's accurate statements about his "other family," his tender obsession with "Dorsey," and how much he missed the little things she did for him? Would it make her heart glad to hear that he still remembered how she had left the light on for him and expected to see its welcoming glow? Would it soothe her soul to know that Derek— her Ted—with his innocently warped sense of time, was still looking for her, yearning to see her face in the window?

Would knowing that Ted was back and surrounded by her family and friends help even a little to heal the hole in her heart, as it did for other mothers who knew their sons were reborn?

Of course I don't know what Doris is thinking or feeling right now, or how she would react. But I do know there are countless people like Doris grieving for a dear child, husband, wife, mother, or father who *is* returned in a new body. Some of these souls in their new incarnations are nearby the very people who grieve for them, intersecting their lives unnoticed, perhaps toddling across the living room when the family gathers at Christmas.

I know this happens, but most people don't see it because they don't know it's possible. I believe that more people could enjoy a surprise reunion with a dearly missed soul if only they could put aside their absolute beliefs, their conviction that "this just doesn't happen," and open to the possibility that maybe it does. A small adjustment in attitude can make all the difference.

After Ted died and reincarnated as Derek, his soul was looking for the light hanging from the garage—that welcoming beacon that connected him to his mother, his home, and the love he left behind. He fully expected it to be there still.

What an apt metaphor for staying open to the possibility of family return. Leave your light on even if you don't know what to believe. Leave your light on to welcome home a loved one returned from heaven.

# Notes

## Chapter 3: *Reincarnation and Biology*

1. The direct address for the forum is *www.Reincarnation Forum.com.*

2. The following work, frequently cited, has been abbreviated *RB:* Ian Stevenson, *Reincarnation and Biology: A Contribution to the Etiology of Birthmarks and Birth Defects,* 2 vols. (Westport, CT: Praeger Publishers, 1997). *RB,* 2: 1429–1442.

3. *RB,* 1: 430–455.

4. Ian Stevenson, *Where Reincarnation and Biology Intersect* (Westport, CT: Praeger Publishers, 1997), 86.

5. *RB,* 2: 1236–1250.

6. Ibid., 1186–1200.

7. *RB,* 1: 300–323.

8. From a lecture titled, "Some of My Journeys in Medicine," given at Southeastern Louisiana University in 1989. The full text is available at *www.childpastlives.org/stevenson.htm.* "What history has taught me is the transience . . . of our ideas about the nature of man. In particular, the history of

medicine shows a humbling succession of ideas about disease, each appearing inviolable for a short period only to prove degradable by the next idea that—at first also hailed an ultimate—is overthrown in its turn. Knowledge in science, as Whitehead said, keeps like fish. ... For me everything now believed by scientists is open to question, and I am always dismayed to find that many scientists accept current knowledge as forever fixed. They confuse the product with the process.

## Chapter 4: *Chicago, USA*

1. In 1983, an article, "American Children Who Claim to Remember Previous Lives," was published in *The Journal of Nervous and Mental Disease*, comparing seventy-nine American cases to 266 cases from India. Although the types of behaviors and number of statements were similar in the two cultures, the American children's statements lacked specifying detail, especially proper names. Out of the seventy-nine American cases, there was only one instance in which the child gave proper names that could identify the previous personality as being someone outside the immediate family. In that one case, it was a former acquaintance of the mother.

2. The Reincarnation Forum is a part of my Web site. We provide it free for discussing any question or idea that has to do with reincarnation, children's past lives, or the work of Dr. Stevenson. Go to *www.ReincarnationForum.com* for the Forum, *www.childpastlives.org* for the whole Web site.

## Chapter 6: *Choosing a Life*

1. Sogyal Rinpoche, *The Tibetan Book of Living and Dying* (New York: HarperCollins, 1994), 290.

2. W. Y. Evans-Wentz, trans., *The Tibetan Book of the Dead* (London: Oxford University Press, 1960), 173.

3. Helen Wambach, *Life Before Life* (New York: Bantam Books, 1979), 56.

4. Ian Stevenson, *Children Who Remember Previous Lives* (Charlottesville: University Press of Virginia, 1987), 68–71.

5. *RB,* 1: 181–197.

6. *RB,* 2: 2076.

7. *RB,* 1: 878.

8. ———. *Twenty Cases Suggestive of Reincarnation* (Charlottesville: University Press of Virginia, 1974), 259–269.

9. ———. *Cases of the Reincarnation Type,* vol. IV (Charlottesville: University Press of Virginia, 1983), 7.

10. Simcha Paull Raphael, *Jewish Views of the Afterlife* (Northvale, NJ: Jason Aronson, Inc., 1994), 394.

11. Winafred Blake Lucas, *Regression Therapy: A Handbook for Professionals,* vol. 2 (Crest Park, CA: Deep Forest Press, 1993), 207.

## Chapter 7: *U-turn in the Womb*

1. Wambach, 99.

2. Michael Newton, *Destiny of Souls* (St. Paul, MN: Llewellyn Publications, 2000), 382.

3. These statistics come by way of Dr. Stevenson. Citing studies of spontaneous abortion: "more conceptuses are lost than develop into born babies. If fertilized eggs that are lost before implantation are included, 'about 52 percent of all pregnancies end before the 28th week, and all but 6 percent of this 52 percent occurs before an abortion is recognized clinically' (A.B. Little, 1998, p. 241). Boklage (1990) stated that 'at least 73 percent of natural single conceptions have no real chance of surviving 6 weeks of gestation. Of the remainder, about 90 percent will survive to term.' "

4. Wambach, 102.

5. *RB,* 1: 1095.

6.    Gladys McGarey, *Born to Live* (Phoenix, AZ: Gabriel Press, 1980), 54–55.

7.    Lucas, 263–264.

8.    Ibid., 299.

## Chapter 8: *Announcing Dreams*

1.    Elisabeth Hallett's Web site is *www.light-hearts.com*

# Bibliography

For more information, see Carol Bowman's Web site: www. childpastlives.org

Anderson, George and Andrew Barone. *Lessons from the Light—Extraordinary Messages of Comfort and Hope from the Other Side.* New York: G. P. Putnam's Sons, 1999.

Evans-Wentz, W. Y., trans. *The Tibetan Book of the Dead.* London: Oxford University Press, 1960.

Guggenheim, Bill and Judy Guggenheim. *Hello from Heaven.* New York: Bantam Books, 1996.

Hallett, Elisabeth. *Soul Trek.* Hamilton, MT: Light Hearts Publishing, 1995.

Head, Joseph and Sylvia Cranston. *Reincarnation: The Phoenix Fire Mystery.* San Diego: Point Loma Publications, 1991.

Kamenetz, Rodger. *The Jew in the Lotus.* New York: Harper-Collins, 1994.

Lucas, Winafred Blake. *Regression Therapy: A Handbook for Professionals, 2 vols.* Crest Park, CA: Deep Forest Press, 1993.

McGarey, Gladys. *Born to Live.* Phoenix: Gabriel Press, 1980.

Available from the author: 7350 E. Stetson Drive, Suite 125, Scottsdale, AZ 85251; 609-946-4544.

Martin, Joel and Patricia Romanowski. *Love Beyond Life—The Healing Power of After-Death Communications.* New York: Dell Publishing, 1997.

Miller, Sukie. *After Death—Mapping the Journey.* New York: Simon and Schuster, 1997.

Moody, Raymond A., Jr.. *Life After Life.* New York: Bantam Books, 1975.

Newton, Michael. *Destiny of Souls.* St. Paul, MN: Llewellyn Publications, 2000.

Newton, Michael. *Journey of Souls.* St. Paul, MN: Llewellyn Publications, 1994.

Raphael, Simcha Paull. *Jewish Views of the Afterlife.* Northvale, New Jersey: Jason Aronson Inc., 1994.

Rinpoche, Sogyal. *The Tibetan Book of Living and Dying.* New York: HarperCollins, 1994.

Stevenson, Ian, M.D. *Cases of the Reincarnation Type, vol. 1, Ten Cases in India.* Charlottesville, VA: University Press of Virginia, 1975.

———. *Cases of the Reincarnation Type, vol. 2, Twelve Cases in Lebanon and Turkey.* Charlottesville, VA: University Press of Virginia, 1980.

———. *Cases of the Reincarnation Type, vol. 4, Twelve Cases in Thailand and Burma.* Charlottesville, VA: University Press of Virginia, 1983.

———. *Children Who Remember Previous Lives.* Charlottesville, VA: University Press of Virginia, 1987.

———. "Phobias in Children Who Claim to Remember Previous Lives." *Journal of Scientific Exploration* 4, no. 2 (1990): 243–254.

————. *Reincarnation and Biology—A Contribution to the Etiology of Birthmarks and Birth Defects,* 2 vols. Westport, CT: Praeger, 1997.

————. *Twenty Cases Suggestive of Reincarnation.* Charlottesville, VA: University Press of Virginia, 1974.

————. *Where Reincarnation and Biology Intersect.* Westport, CT: Praeger, 1997.

TenDam, Hans. *Exploring Reincarnation.* London: Arkana (The Penguin Group), 1990. Out of print.

Van Praagh, James. *Reaching to Heaven.* New York: Dutton, 1999.

————.*Talking to Heaven.* New York: Dutton, 1997.

Wambach, Helen. *Life Before Life.* New York: Bantam, 1979. Out of print.

Weiss, Brian. *Many Lives, Many Masters.* New York: Simon & Schuster, 1988.

————. *Messages from the Masters.* New York: Warner Books, 2000.

————. *Only Love Is Real.* New York: Warner Books, 1996.

————. *Through Time into Healing.* New York: Simon & Schuster, 1992.

Whitton, Joel and Joe Fisher. *Life Between Life.* New York: Warner Books, 1986.

Williamson, Linda. *Children and the Spirit World.* London: Piatkus, 1997.

Woolger, Roger. *Other Lives, Other Selves.* New York: Doubleday, 1987. Woolger is one of the leading theorists and practitioners of past life therapy. A must-read.

Wendy Sherman

Ambassador